DANCE *of the* TRILLIONS

*Providing new perspectives and
knowledge on an increasingly complex,
uncertain, and interconnected world.*

The Chatham House Insights Series
Series Editor: Caroline Soper

The Insights series provides new perspectives on and knowledge about an increasingly complex, uncertain, and interconnected world. Concise, lively, and authoritative, these books explore, through different modes of interpretation, a wide range of country, regional, and international developments, all within a global context. Focusing on topical issues in key policy areas, such as health, security, economics, law, and the environment, volumes in the series will be written accessibly by leading experts—both academic and practitioner—to anticipate trends and illuminate new ideas and thinking. Insights books will be of great interest to all those seeking to develop a deeper understanding of the policy challenges and choices facing decision makers, including academics, practitioners, and general readers.

Published or forthcoming titles:

Amitai Etzioni, *Foreign Policy: Thinking Outside the Box* (2016)

Keir Giles, *Moscow Rules: How Russia Works, and
What It Means for the West* (forthcoming)

Nigel Gould-Davies, *Global Risk in an Age of Transformation* (forthcoming)

Chatham House, the Royal Institute of International Affairs, is a world-leading policy institute based in London. Its mission is to help governments and societies build a sustainably secure, prosperous, and just world.

Chatham House does not express opinions of its own. The opinions expressed in this publication are the responsibility of the author(s).

DANCE

of the

TRILLIONS

Developing Countries and Global Finance

DAVID LUBIN

BROOKINGS INSTITUTION PRESS
Washington, D.C.

CHATHAM HOUSE
The Royal Institute of International Affairs
London

Library of Congress Cataloging-in-Publication data are available.
ISBN 978-0-8157-3674-5 (pbk : alk. paper)
ISBN 978-0-8157-3664-6 (ebook)

9 8 7 6 5 4 3 2 1

Typeset in Adobe Garamond

Composition by Elliott Beard

In memory of Donald and Gloria

Contents

Contents

Acknowledgments

I am very grateful to Robin Niblett, who kindly allowed me to attach myself to Chatham House as a Visiting Fellow during the months that I worked on this book, and to Andrew Pitt, who with equal kindness allowed me to detach myself from my day job at Citi during the same period.

Michel Nies was exceptionally helpful in providing me with data and analysis to support what I have written here. Sebastian Mallaby's comments on my draft improved it considerably, as did Jake Statham's careful editing. I would also like to thank Samiran Chakraborty, Johanna Chua, Pete Dattels, Fernando Diaz, Gene Frieda, Nigel Gould-Davies, Donato Guarino, Anurag Jha, Peter Jones, Piotr Kalisz, James Kynge, Catherine Mann, Felix Martin, Siddharth Mathur, Amanda Moss, Ernesto Revilla, Caroline Soper, Ivan Tchakarov, Ekaterina Vlasova, Adam Ward, and Jonathan Wheatley for their comments, discussions, and help at various stages of this project. I am also very grateful to Willem Buiter and Hélène Rey for their encouragement.

And to Tamara, Daniel, and Hannah, I owe much more than thanks. To them I owe everything.

Introduction

What's Past Is Prologue

In the summer of 1920, Havana must have felt like the throbbing heart of civilization. Its main thoroughfare, the Prado, was as packed with cars as Fifth Avenue in New York, as Rolls-Royces and Pierce Arrows flowed along the tree-lined boulevard. The world-famous tenor Enrico Caruso, in the twilight of his career, was paid $10,000 for each performance during a Cuban tour.[1] Farmers came to town to spend money in the city's jewelry shops. All in all, the ashes of the Great War seemed to dust off easily that summer in the Caribbean, revealing a shiny confidence about the future.

This heady economic boom came to be named, after a 1916 musical production that had toured Havana, the "Dance of the Millions." At the root of the boom was an explosion in sugar prices that catapulted Cuba toward wealth that could otherwise only have been dreamed of. Wartime controls on the price of sugar had been gradually lifted toward the end of 1918, and Cuba was the country most surely in a position to take advantage of this, as its sugar production had increased substantially during the war years: by 1918 the country's sugar output was some 3.4 million metric tonnes, a million tonnes higher than its prewar level.

Outside Cuba, war-related changes in the global sugar market were also

1

working in Cuba's favor. The war had destroyed the sugar beet fields of
Germany and Austria-Hungary, and Europe's sugar output had shriveled.
This allowed the Cuban Sugar Cane Corporation to emerge as the biggest
sugar company in the world. The war's end had also helped trigger a surge
in the demand for sugar, not least because of the January 1919 ratification
of the Eighteenth Amendment in the United States: the prohibition of alco-
hol pushed U.S. consumers toward sugar-based soft drinks in a way never
before seen, and per capita consumption of soft drinks in the United States
rose from nineteen bottles in 1914 to thirty-eight bottles in 1919.

The rise in sugar prices during 1919 took on a bizarre quality. In a country where a sugar price of 5½ cents per pound was considered enough to
"stimulate the island to extreme prosperity,"[2] the price rose to 10 cents in
March that year, to 15½ cents in early April, and to 22½ cents on May 19.

The boom in sugar begat a boom in finance. During the first half of
1920, the total assets of the Banco Nacional, Cuba's largest bank, increased
by 66 percent, and those of the Banco Español, Cuba's oldest bank, by 33
percent.[3] This sudden increase in the availability of credit was considerably
bolstered by an inflow of funds from American banks: National City Bank
opened twenty-two branches in Cuba in 1919 alone, taking advantage of
the 1913 Federal Reserve Act, which had lifted restrictions on U.S. banks'
international expansion.[4] Bankers must have been in a state of high excite-
ment about the ability to secure loans on sugar crops whose value could
reach untold heights. After all, if the price of sugar had doubled in just a
few spring months of 1919, why couldn't it double again? And again? In a
frenzy of financial activity, some fifty sugar mills, more than one quarter of
the 198 existing in Cuba, were acquired by new owners in 1919 and 1920.[5]

Yet dollars flowed to Cuba not just because they were pulled there by the
spectacular improvement in Cuba's terms of trade. They were also pushed.
Monetary conditions in the United States had grown exceptionally loose
during the war. The newly formed U.S. Federal Reserve had lent freely to
U.S. banks to help support their purchases of war bonds. This Fed lending
at low interest rates eased credit conditions and caused inflation to rise. So
the inflation-adjusted return from lending within the United States went
down, and that helped push U.S. capital to Cuba. Inflation-adjusted interest rates in the United States were very substantially negative at this time: in
June 1919 the Fed's policy rate was only 4 percent, while the inflation rate
that month was 15 percent. No wonder foreign lending looked attractive!

But just as loose U.S. monetary policy had pushed American capital toward Cuba at the war's end, U.S. monetary tightening helped pull it back. In December 1919 the Fed's policy interest rate was raised to 4¾ percent and reached 7 percent by June 1920 as the Fed struggled to gain control over an inflation rate that, by midyear, had topped 24 percent. Although the Fed's policy rate remained highly negative in real terms, the raising of nominal interest rates was enough to worsen the climate for capital flows to Cuba.

Meanwhile, European beet production recovered in late 1920, and the U.S. economy was beginning a decline—helped along by the Fed's tightening—that turned into recession the following year. As a result, sugar prices started to fall, and by the autumn of 1920 Cuba's boom was turning to bust. By Christmas of 1920 the price of sugar had dropped to 3¾ cents a pound. The result: widespread bank failures in Cuba, the takeover of many Cuban-owned mills by U.S. creditors, and a moratorium on international payments declared by the Cuban government on October 11.[6] An economic collapse followed this with an inevitability that would become all too familiar to developing countries at numerous points in the century that followed.

This book aims to set out the story of what makes money flow from big, high-income countries to lower-income countries, and what makes it flow out again. In Cuba's case, the cast of actors included a boom in commodity prices influenced by a big change in the geopolitical environment, a loosening of monetary conditions in the United States that helped push capital toward riskier borrowers in foreign countries in a search for higher returns, and innovation within financial markets that facilitated the international mobility of capital. And it included what John Kenneth Galbraith called "a kind of sophisticated stupidity" that pushed both lenders and borrowers into a hubristic failure to understand that the future might not be as rosy as the present.[7]

These themes will reappear throughout this book. Most important, though, Cuba's "Dance of the Millions" helps illustrate how delicate the relationship between developing countries and international finance can be. A century on, we are still searching for an answer to this question: how can developing countries interact with global capital markets in a way that generates stability and growth rather than volatility and crisis? This book traces how the answer to that question has shifted uncomfortably during the past fifty years, and how it might evolve in the future.

And, in altered form, Cuba's "Dance of the Millions" gives this book its title. One of the quaint pleasures available to the economic historian is how what used to be considered a big number can seem, by today's standards, laughably small. By one estimate the world's entire stock of international indebtedness in 1932 was around $50 billion.[8] These days $50 billion would just about buy you the external debt of Morocco. A better estimate of the current stock of international indebtedness in 2018 is closer to $90 trillion, of which around $25 trillion is owed by developing countries. "Dance of the Trillions" seems a more apt way of capturing the scale of finance in the modern era, during which the size and volatility of capital flows to developing countries have been unprecedented. And that stock of debt can only have risen to such giddy heights because of globalization, and the unique role that finance has played in opening and interconnecting markets.

From Globalization to Globalism

Historical episodes of globalization come and go. The first modern era of globalization stretched from the 1850s to the early 1930s, though with an extended hiatus around World War I. A second era dates from the early 1970s. Like the earlier era, the recent era of globalization can be simply described as a surge in the international mobility of goods, services, people, and finance. But unlike its predecessor, the current phase of globalization has been a gift to developing countries. In the late nineteenth and early twentieth centuries, industrialization visited only the developed world; India, China, and the rest of the developing world stayed poor. By contrast, the modern era of globally integrated markets has seen developing countries benefit above all.

To understand this, we need only consider the simple phenomenon of "income convergence": are developing countries closing the gap between their average incomes and those in the developed world? For nearly the whole of the twentieth century—until, that is, the benefits of modern globalization became evident—developing countries' per capita income kept falling in comparison to per capita income in the developed world. India is a good example. In the 1920s, India's income per capita was around 15 percent of that in Western Europe and the United States. By the 1980s, after two generations of "deconvergence," Indians' average income had fallen to 6 percent of that in the developed world. It is only during the recent era of globalization that India has seen its average per capita income increase in comparison to that of more advanced economies: it was around 13 percent in the 2010s.[9] Data for Latin America tell a similar story, though that continent's catch-up only really dates from the early 2000s.

In other words, economic catch-up for developing countries is a recent thing, and it can only be understood as the consequence of the gradual integration of global markets for goods, services, assets, and inputs since the 1970s. Without income convergence, it is impossible to imagine that the phrase "emerging markets"—the marketing term that evolved in the late 1980s to describe those developing countries that, at any given time, have access to international finance—could have been coined, or that the concept it embodied could have become an organizing principle within international capital markets.

"Emerging markets" is an odd expression—a country is more than a mere market—and this book defaults to referring to "developing countries," a label with a longer history and one that fits more naturally across the span of time under scrutiny here. That said, defining either "developing countries" or "emerging markets" with anything like precision is not straightforward. Overall, two concepts are relevant. The first is growth: developing countries either can or do grow more rapidly than developed countries—at least, they typically have done so in the modern era of globalization. And the second is risk: a developing country is more likely to have what is sometimes described as "institutional weakness"—whereby the rule of law may not be fully entrenched, political stability may not be taken for granted, the effectiveness of government and the transparency of decision making may be low, and trust in financial intermediation might be weak. Of course, these weaknesses can often feature in developed countries, too, but the difference can be summarized in the idea that developing countries, from a creditor's perspective, are "higher-yielding," offering returns that can't be captured in more advanced economies. That higher return can reflect either better growth prospects or a risk premium, and often both.

And it is this prospect of higher yield that helps to define "emerging markets" as an asset class in international capital markets. These days, the asset class is captured in benchmark indices that reflect the performance of a group of markets against which institutional investors measure their own investment prowess. The list of countries included in these indices, both in the bond and equity markets, is rather limited: the MSCI Emerging Markets Index for equity investors includes Brazil, Chile, Colombia, Mexico, Peru, the Czech Republic, Egypt, Greece, Poland, Hungary, Qatar, Russia, South Africa, Turkey, the United Arab Emirates, China, India, Indonesia, Korea, Malaysia, Pakistan, the Philippines, Taiwan, and Thailand. J.P. Morgan's EMBI Global Index of dollar-denominated bonds has a longer list of countries that includes, for example, Belize, Cameroon, Georgia, Honduras, Jamaica, Iraq, Tunisia, and Zambia—sixty-five in all.

In any case, what's important to understand is that the notion of emerging markets couldn't exist without globalization. And in the modern era, globalization has, in some ways, been a creation of the spread of finance. The foundations for this era were laid in the 1970s, and those foundations were largely financial: this was the decade that gave developing countries, for the first time in forty years, access to loans from the international banking system. As the decades proceeded, the edifice took on a more coherent shape. In the 1980s, the inward-looking development strategies that many countries had followed in previous decades were ditched in favor of outward-looking policies. Trade barriers were dismantled, the state retreated from its formerly dominant role in economic activity, and investment flows were encouraged. This was, on its own terms, spectacularly successful: adjusted for inflation, some 90 percent of the entire stock of foreign direct investment (FDI) in developing countries was created after 1990. And in the 1990s, the collapse of communism helped integrate a swath of the world's population into a more globally connected economy and created room for an unprecedented rise in the global movement of people. In 2000, one in thirty-five people of the world's population was living outside his or her country of birth; the ratio in 1910 was only one in forty-eight people.[10]

From the late 1990s, two developments brought the phenomenon of emerging markets to a much wider audience of investors. The first was the boom in commodity prices. Between 2001 and 2011, global commodity prices rose in inflation-adjusted terms for the second-longest period since the late eighteenth century.[11] And the second was a kind of hyperglobalization of world trade. During the fifteen years between 1992 and 2006, just before the global financial crisis, the average growth rate in global trade volumes was just under 7 percent—more than twice the rate of real global GDP growth, which was just over 3 percent. The twentieth century had never seen anything like this explosion in global trade. The crucial player in this development was China. Neither of these booms—in commodity prices or in world trade—would have been remotely conceivable without China's economic rise.

During this period, "globalization" became "globalism": an economic phenomenon became a philosophy. As a philosophy, globalism can be described as the idea that the international integration of the markets for goods, labor, and capital is an unquestionably good thing, that the balance between global governance and national sovereignty should be tipped toward the former, and that the balance between states and markets should be tipped toward the latter.

Two features of globalism need emphasizing. The first is the extent to which it has been a U.S.-shaped phenomenon: its contours have been influenced by Washington to create a financial world more in sync with Washington's values and in its own interests. How could it be otherwise when the most famous organizing concept in economic policy during this period was called the "Washington Consensus"? This phrase, coined by the British economist John Williamson at a conference in 1989, originally captured the idea that ten policies commanded a high degree of respect among the Washington-based institutions—the International Monetary Fund, the World Bank—and the U.S. Treasury. These were to keep budget deficits small, spend public money wisely, keep tax rates low and the tax base high, allow the market to determine interest rates, let the exchange rate be competitive, reduce barriers to trade, let in FDI, privatize state enterprises, abolish regulations that restrict competition, and provide secure property rights.[12]

While Williamson's original version of the Washington Consensus doesn't say much about liberalizing capital flows—except for FDI—it is safe to say that Washington's general view about the international mobility of capital in the 1980s and 1990s was that it was more or less unequivocally good. During those decades and beyond, the IMF, the World Bank, and the U.S. Treasury encouraged countries to eschew controls on inflows and outflows of capital. Even in the early 2000s the U.S. Treasury was insisting, for example, that Korea and Chile abandon any ability to use capital controls as a price for signing free-trade agreements with the United States.[13]

And this underlines the second critical feature of globalism: a neglect of, or complacency toward, the oversized role played by finance. Consider the following. In 1970, the value of developing countries' trade was equal to around 22 percent of their GDP. By 2015, that share had risen to the equivalent of around 58 percent. That's a reasonable measure of how emerging economies became more connected to international markets for goods, a kind of "entry-level" definition of globalization. But the growth of finance was explosive in comparison. In 1970 the stock of international assets and liabilities on developing countries' balance sheets—their "international investment position"—was equivalent to around 30 percent of their GDP. By 2015, that figure had risen to 165 percent of GDP.[14] Financial integration galloped way faster and way further than trade during the modern era of globalization.

The idea of giving developing countries access to international capital markets is, at some level, undeniably a good one. Without access to external financing, a developing country—indeed, any country—is limited to fending for itself, effectively in a state of autarky. With access to international capital, though, governments, firms, and households can stretch their buying power, getting access to goods, services, technology, and ideas that otherwise would be unavailable.

At its most basic, the availability of external financing creates the possibility of running a trade deficit—or, more broadly speaking, a deficit on the current account of the balance of payments. This occurs when the sum of a country's spending on imports of foreign goods and services (including transfers, such as grants to other countries and foreign workers' remittances to their home countries) is greater than the income it receives for goods and services that it exports (as well as income on foreign investments, inward remittances from expatriate workers, and so on).

Economics textbooks define a country's current account balance as the difference between savings and investment in the economy. A current account surplus indicates that savings exceed investment; a deficit indicates the opposite. Since investment spending is needed to support growth, the availability of external financing should in principle help countries grow, because it gives space for both the private sector and the public sector in an economy to spend more than they earn. This doesn't necessarily translate into enhanced economic growth prospects, of course: borrowing merely to finance consumption won't have the same effect as borrowing to finance investment in new machinery, for example. Or, a bit more technically, if a current account deficit reflects a decline in savings rather than an increase in investment, that deficit is unlikely to be doing much to benefit the economy in the long term. But in principle, the availability of external finance offers the hope of freedom from a state of pure national self-dependence.

Capital Mobility and Its Discontents

Somewhere along the line, though, international finance in our era of globalization somehow seemed to turn from slave to master.

Put simply, the track record of fully liberalized capital flows during the modern era of globalization is not a happy one. The incidence of banking crises and currency crises globally has been much higher since the early 1970s than in the "preglobalization" postwar Bretton Woods era, and there seems to be little evidence that an indiscriminate opening up of one's economy to all forms of capital has had much of a positive impact on growth or welfare in developing countries.[15] Of course, that isn't the same as saying that globalization has had no effect on growth or welfare. It has, but those effects have come largely from FDI, from trade, and from China's surging influence in the global economy. Indeed, China and India are near-perfect examples of how very strong economic performance in developing countries needn't have much to do with open capital accounts: both these countries have rather closed ones. In managing that trick, their experience neatly sums up the difference between economic globalization and financial globalization.

The failure of fully liberalized capital flows has come into focus slowly over the last twenty years. This might seem odd in light of the fact that the 1980s and 1990s were peppered with financial crises in developing countries. From Mexico's default in the summer of 1982 through to Argentina's default in December 2001, developing countries suffered a succession of crises that lasted a full two decades. There is a direct link between Latin America's debt crisis in the 1980s, Mexico's "Tequila" crisis in 1994, Asia's crises in 1997, Russia's crisis in 1998, Brazil's in 1999, Turkey's in 2001, and Argentina's in December 2001.

These crises didn't by themselves demonstrate the failure of liberalized capital flows. Indeed, the conventional analysis at the time was that these crises happened in countries where policymakers simply tried to have their economic cake and eat it: they sought to maintain both fixed exchange rates and independent monetary policy in a world of globalized capital flows—the "impossible trinity," as it is often described. Either that, or they had simply borrowed money irresponsibly. The problem, in other words, wasn't global financial volatility per se but rather the failure of countries to equip themselves properly to deal with that volatility or to run sensible enough policies to make good use of external financing. In very rough economic weather, so the analysis ran, developing countries just weren't wearing warm enough clothes.

So policymakers in developing countries drew two lessons from the 1980s and 1990s, neither of which really encouraged them to close their capital accounts or impose restrictions on highly mobile "hot money" inflows. The first lesson was that crises resulted from weak balance sheets. Above all, this meant that countries had too few of the reserves of foreign exchange that central banks could sell during periods of capital outflow to stabilize their economies, but, as we shall see, it also meant that governments needed to put a lid on the growth of public debt. The second lesson was to avoid fixing, or trying to manage, their exchange rates. In a world where the balance of power was moving away from policymakers and toward markets, a form of power struggle took place between governments and traders over the question of who should be in control of setting the price of a developing country's currency. By the end of the 1990s that question had been settled: it was the job of markets, not governments, to decide what the price of a dollar should be.

And so the 2000s, for the most part, saw policymakers in the developing world relying less on the fixing of exchange rates and more on the accumulation of foreign exchange reserves as a form of self-insurance. More than that: this period was characterized by an intense focus by policymakers in developing countries on the need to have strong balance sheets, not just by keeping stocks of foreign reserves high but also by keeping public debt burdens low. In 1987 the average ratio of government debt to GDP for developing countries was 75 percent; by 2008, this had fallen to 34 percent. This was their version of "dressing up warmly." But one of the central questions asked in the chapters that follow is this: what was the cost of all this effort to insulate economies from external shocks and keep balance sheets strong?

Did it mean that policymakers in developing countries paid less attention to other reforms that might have been more important in supporting growth? This is a difficult question to answer, but it is tempting to argue that the answer is yes.

Sometimes, how warmly you dress isn't the issue; sometimes it is simply that the weather is just too cold to be outdoors. In the same way, the world has gradually come to understand that unrestricted international capital mobility may be a problem that no reasonable amount of self-insurance can protect against. Global capital flows can contaminate developing countries with financial fragility, as though some bacteria in the waters of international finance made it dangerous to drink.

One way of expressing this problem is that there is a sort of global financial "weather" cycle that creates downpours and droughts in external financing, and that this cycle isn't easily managed even by allowing your currency to float freely in a way that, in principle, ought to help accommodate different climates. Developing countries in particular may just be the passive victims of these swings, their monetary policies and the direction of their economies more or less at the mercy of even small changes in the amount of risk that suppliers of capital in rich countries wish to take on.[16] This helps make the argument that there may just be no way that developing countries could make themselves safe short of trying to restrict capital inflows by taxing them, or imposing regulatory requirements that limit investors' ability to make an abrupt dash for the exit.

Although controls on capital inflows had been briefly fashionable in the early 1990s, it was only really after 2009 that a number of countries started to assemble a range of tools to prevent capital entering in the first place. Brazil set the pace in October 2009 by raising its IOF tax on bond and equity inflows, and a variety of measures were subsequently introduced by China, Colombia, Indonesia, Korea, Peru, the Philippines, and Taiwan. And while capital controls in the early 1990s had been considered racy, their use has now moved beyond controversy. By the end of 2012 the IMF itself was arguing that "capital flow management measures can be useful."[17] And that's because it has seemed blindingly obvious, at various points during the past few years, that much of the foreign money entering developing countries was speculative in nature, highly reversible, and contributing little to proper capital formation in these countries.

Other factors have also helped to soften the Washington Consensus view about international capital mobility. One is the absence of any evidence that countries that did choose to restrict capital inflows suffered much as a result of that choice. Another is the apparently endless increase in the sheer scale of global finance. And a third is China.

It is difficult to avoid hyperbole in describing the economic effect that China has had on the developing world in the past fifteen years. Commodity-exporting countries in the developing world saw their terms of trade dramatically affected by the way China reshaped the global demand for commodities. Manufacturing-based economies too saw their industrial structures revolutionized by the way China established itself as a central node in geographically disaggregated production chains. And the sheer weight of the Chinese economy has increased dramatically. Between 2002 and 2006, China accounted for 15 percent of global GDP growth. Ten years on, between 2012 and 2016, China's contribution to global GDP growth had reached 36 percent; the U.S. contribution was half that.

So the global economy has grown emphatically more "China shaped," for developing countries above all. And this is not just economic influence but financial, too: China is becoming rapidly more relevant to developing countries as a supplier of external funding.

Where economic and financial power lead, intellectual influence follows. Just as U.S. economic dominance created a U.S.-shaped era of globalization, an emerging China will increasingly take part in a process that will make the international financial system more shaped by China: less Washington Consensus and more Beijing Consensus.

What might a China-shaped international financial system look like? At the very least, it will be one that changes the balance of power between states and markets. What China wants to do, over time, is to gently reassert the role of the state in shaping the international monetary order. The order that arose from the ashes of the burnt-out Bretton Woods regime in the 1970s—dominated by free markets, in which floating exchange rates and fully open capital accounts became fashionable—is not one that China feels comfortable in.

A pretty clear expression of China's view was delivered in April 2015, when Zhou Xiaochuan, the country's central bank governor, defined a concept he described as "managed convertibility," discussed more fully in chapter 5. China wants to keep hold of discretionary powers to limit speculative capital flows, and wants to restrict capital movements in order to deal with balance-of-payments problems. For China it is the policymaker, not the market, who should have the final say in deciding which capital movements are good and which are bad. In other words, China's view on these issues fits quite neatly with the evolving consensus that unrestricted capital mobility may not be such a great thing after all.

If China continues in its effort to change the balance of power between states and markets in shaping the role of international finance in the global economy, one would do well to bear in mind the historical see-sawing on this question. The reason why the 1970s saw the beginning of market-oriented globalization is that the state-driven regime that preceded it—the Bretton Woods era—failed. And the reason why the Bretton Woods era came into existence can be traced back to a high level of discomfort with the consequences of unrestricted capital mobility in the 1920s and 1930s.

Back to the Future, Part 1: The 1930s and Its Echoes

Oversized finance was widely thought to lie behind the failure of globalism in the 1930s. Indeed, the idea that too much global capital mobility was at the root of the world economy's problems became so entrenched that it formed the entire basis of the post-1945 Bretton Woods system, whose essential aim was to create a liberal order for global trade while restricting capital movements. As early as 1933, John Maynard Keynes, the indispensable author of the Bretton Woods regime, had become convinced of the need to squeeze capital flows, writing, "I sympathize, therefore, with those who would minimize, rather than with those who would maximize, economic entanglements between nations. Ideas, knowledge, art, hospitality, travel—these are things which should of their nature be international. But let goods be homespun whenever it is reasonably and conveniently possible, and, above all, *let finance be primarily national.*"[18]

How did capital flows get such a bad name in the 1930s? The answer lies in the way the global economy was reconstructed after World War I, and in the coming of age of the United States as the engine of the global financial system. Cuba's Dance of the Millions in the early 1920s was just an early warning of what would become a crisis of more systemic proportions.

Just as the Napoleonic Wars had turned London into the capital of European finance, World War I established New York as the financial capital of the world. The war turned the United States from a net international debtor into a net creditor. This was partly built on the fact that U.S. exporters fared particularly well during the conflict: foreign sales of agriculture rose thanks to the devastation of Europe, and U.S. cars enjoyed steadily rising foreign demand. And on the back of this, the United States became the world's provider of international liquidity. At the same time, the war also gave birth to financial innovations that greased the wheels of international lending. Under the Liberty Loan Act of 1917, the U.S. Treasury bought securities of foreign governments that were at war with enemies of the United States. Those purchases of foreign securities were financed by sales of dollar-denominated securities to the American public in matching amounts. As one account put it at the time, "Millions of individuals who had never clipped a coupon or owned a share of stock now became 'investment-minded' for the first time in their lives."[19]

For American bondholders, lending money to poorer countries abroad looked almost irresistible. During the whole of the 1920s, the average yield on a portfolio of sixty high-grade U.S. corporate bonds was 4.94 percent, while the average yield on new foreign bonds during that period was 6.59 percent: a spread of 165 basis points.[20] Between 1922 and 1928, some $2 billion worth of Latin American bonds alone were sold to investors in the United States.[21]

This was an age of aggressive financial expansion. Thanks to the liberalizing effects of the 1913 Federal Reserve Act, banks vastly increased the number of their international operations and opened foreign branches to win underwriting mandates from countries unknown to most U.S. investors. American bond salesmen used picture books to introduce investors to unfamiliar foreign parts.[22] More than thirty U.S. investment banks competed to win a mandate from the city of Budapest to underwrite its bonds; fourteen competed over Belgrade. A village in Bavaria looking for $125,000 found itself convinced to borrow $3 million.[23]

The British perspective on all this was that U.S. bond salesmen and their clients were overexcited neophytes. Commenting in the years following the inevitable crisis, Chatham House authors weightily (and somewhat hypocritically) intoned that British investors would have been a more stable source of funds for countries in Latin America and Eastern Europe, since the British investing public "had been accustomed for generations to regard overseas loans as one of the main channels for the investment of its savings."[24]

And the crisis came. Two shocks hit countries in Latin America and elsewhere from 1928 onward: a collapse in commodity prices and a simultaneous collapse in cross-border lending. By late 1929, agricultural prices were around 30 percent lower than they had been in 1925. By December 1930, prices were down 60 percent from their 1925 level, and they were down 75 percent by the end of 1932. This decline in commodity prices helped to cause a decline in cross-border lending—why continue to lend to borrowers suffering from falling incomes?—which in turn intensified the economic crisis. In any case, foreign lending had come to a natural halt in mid-1928 because the U.S. stock market's rise made it seem so much more enticing for investors than, say, buying Colombian bonds. This cutoff in foreign lending didn't cause immediate panic since investors remained confident that an appetite for bonds would return.[25] But given time, the choking-off of international finance proved fatal: the availability of dollars declined just as the need for funding increased because of governments' dependence on commodity prices to support fiscal revenues.

Defaults followed. The first was Bolivia in December 1930, followed by Peru in March 1931; Chile, Colombia, and Cuba came thereafter. By 1934, the only Latin American economy of any significance that had kept current on its debt payments was Argentina. Argentina survived largely because it showed more willingness to let its currency weaken in response to lower commodity prices.

In the opinion of Chatham House at the time: "A central feature of the depression was the exchange difficulties with which many countries were confronted; and in these exchange difficulties the large sums required to meet the external debt service were a major factor. . . . It is now generally accepted that the international lending of the period in question only eased the difficulties of the moment at the expense of greatly aggravating them in subsequent years."[26]

So the intellectual consensus of the 1930s was that much of the blame for the Great Depression could be laid at the door of international capital mobility. The money that came in inevitably went out. One version of this argument was that floating exchange rates and capital mobility were in-consistent with free international trade. If international capital movements destabilize currencies, that would inevitably encourage beggar-thy-neighbor trade policies because country *x* would use an import tariff to protect itself against country *y*'s currency depreciation.

In other words, international capital mobility was identified as a central weakness during the first era of globalization, which came to an ugly halt in the early 1930s. And if finance was a problem back then, no wonder it has been accused of being so during the modern era of globalization, in light of the growth of the financial sector since the 1970s! What goes around, comes around. Just as the failures of globalization in the early twentieth century led to a rediscovery of the role of the public sector in restricting market ac-tivity, it is possible to argue that we are beginning to see something similar today, with China at the center of this shift.

Because what's past is prologue, or at least can be, the structure of this book is largely chronological.

- Chapter 1 looks at the 1970s, which saw developing countries gain access, for the first time since the 1930s, to measurable inflows of capital from international financial markets. This chapter focuses on three aspects of the story: the role that markets played, through "petrodollar recycling," in allocating capital from surplus countries to those with deficits; the importance of global inflation in under-standing capital movements during the 1970s; and the way in which the 1970s lending boom turned to bust, thanks largely to the U.S. Fed's effort to defeat inflation in the early 1980s. It would take almost a generation for developing countries to adapt themselves to a new reality: the overwhelming influence of U.S. monetary policy in their economic life.

- Chapter 2 examines the two decades of crisis that followed this, and draws connections between Latin America's "lost decade" of the 1980s and the string of emerging markets crises that stretched across the 1990s and early 2000s. The lesson of these decades was that weak bal-ance sheets and pegged exchange rates created unmanageable vulner-abilities in a world of globalized capital flows. Since the international financial system would not be made "safe" for developing countries, they had to ensure their own safety within the international financial system.

- Chapter 3 addresses the question of how, despite these crises, "emerging markets" became more coherent as an investment theme during the past thirty years. The chapter emphasizes the difference between economic globalization and financial globalization and examines the way developing countries strengthened their balance sheets to protect themselves against the volatility of capital flows.

- Chapter 4 examines the rise of China since the early 2000s as a more decisive influence on the economic life of developing countries. It assesses how China's rise helped support a long string of current account surpluses in the developing world, adding a further source of financial protection to those countries.

- Chapter 5 looks to the future by investigating whether the rise of China's economic and financial power could be translated into intellectual influence over the way developing countries manage their capital accounts and their economic policies. It discusses China's rejection of full capital account openness and its determination to use discretion to manage capital flows. It argues that if the future of global capital mobility is influenced by Beijing, that future will more likely resemble a Bretton Woods–type world than the one we are currently in.

The basic arc of this book, therefore, follows the move in the relationship between developing countries and international finance from a U.S.-shaped regime to a China-shaped one. The emergence in the 1970s of a U.S.-dominated financial system gave more space to markets to allocate capital, and increasingly more space to a rule: that global capital should be allowed to move freely. Moving toward a China-shaped world, on the other hand, implies a bigger role for the state—as a source of funding and as an economic agent—and more room for policymakers' discretion to replace the use of rules. In a funny sort of way, that kind of world would resemble in certain ways the one that followed the last collapse of globalization in the 1930s. So it really does seem that what's past is prologue.

ONE

Enter Finance

The 1970s

JEDDAH, 1974

"What are the Arabs going to do with it all?" asked *The Economist* in its first issue of 1974. The "it" was dollars, and plenty of them. By 1973 Saudi Arabia had established itself as the "swing" producer in international oil markets, giving it overwhelming control over the supply, and hence the price, of crude. Late that year, the kingdom had used this dominance to explosive effect: on October 16, ten days after Egyptian forces crossed the Suez Canal and launched the Arab-Israeli War, the Saudi-dominated Organization of the Petroleum Exporting Countries (OPEC) announced in Kuwait City that the posted price of oil would rise from $3.01 per barrel to $5.11. Four days later, on October 20—the day after President Richard Nixon announced a $2.2 billion military aid package for Israel—Saudi Arabia cut off all shipments of oil to the United States. Other Arab states followed suit, and by January 1974 the price of oil had risen to over $10 per barrel.

This decisive display of seller's power led to a peacetime redistribution of global wealth on a scale that hadn't been seen in living memory. In 1973 the world's major oil exporters collectively had a current account surplus of around $6.7 billion, equivalent to around 0.5 percent of U.S. GDP. Within a year, that surplus had grown tenfold, to $69 billion, closer to 4.5 percent of U.S. GDP. For the rest of the world, the staggering scale of this transfer of financial resources to oil producers delivered three shocks: a huge deterioration in the trade balances of oil-importing countries, surging inflation, and the collapse of one of the pillars of the world economy, namely, low-cost energy from petroleum.

These are the shocks that gave birth to an era that allowed developing countries, or less developed countries (LDCs), as they were christened then, to regain measurable access to international financial markets for the first time since the 1930s. Memories of that decade had died with the generation that presided over the Depression-era defaults. A new, more confident generation of financiers, with balance sheets empty of any exposure to developing countries, had emerged. And the rules by which these financiers played were made in America. As we will see, the "petrodollar recycling" of the 1970s was governed by U.S. banks and supported by the U.S. government; and it responded to incentives shaped by U.S. monetary policy.

From an arithmetical point of view, the simplest solution to the sudden rise in the surpluses of the oil exporters would have been simply for them to spend those surpluses, creating a source of new demand for the goods and services produced by stricken oil importers. But arithmetic couldn't, in this case, stretch its logic to the real world: the suddenness and size of the increase in oil exporters' wealth made this impossible, since the economies of the oil-exporting countries lacked the capacity to spend at a rate even close to that at which they were accumulating wealth. Saudi Arabia's current account surplus in 1974 was an incredible 51 percent of GDP: it is impossible to imagine a surplus of this scale being spent on goods and services from the rest of the world in a short time.

So a rise in foreign assets, not a rise in spending on foreign goods, was the most obvious consequence of the oil exporters' gambit in 1973. But that left a couple of questions unanswered. If the petrodollars newly arrived on the balance sheets of Arab and other oil-exporting countries needed to go somewhere to earn a return, where would that be? And by what means would they travel?

Answering the first question was pretty straightforward: the surpluses generated by the oil shock would naturally find a home in financing the current account deficits of oil-importing countries burdened by the rise in energy prices. The only visible alternative to this would be misery for oil importers: if they were unable to export their way out of their trade deficits, the only response to the oil shock other than borrowing to pay for it would be to cut domestic spending in order to shrink those deficits. In the context of the early 1970s, though, this was more or less unthinkable. The aftermath of World War II had seen a pleasant surge in global economic activity that, if possible, no one wanted to bring to an end. And for developing countries in particular, the political imperative for strong growth was irresistible. Brazil, for example, had been enjoying what became known as its *milagre econômico*, an economic "miracle" period of exceptionally rapid growth under the military government of Emilio Médici that saw the economy take off from 1968 onward. That miracle was partly the result of increased foreign borrowing by the Brazilian government. So if the existence of petrodollars allowed even more borrowing in a way that would help sustain growth, how could this be a bad idea? That argument also coincided with a moral one: how could anybody defend the proposition that the world's poorest countries pay for the oil shock with low growth?

But if it was pretty obviously expedient to "recycle" the petrodollars in the form of lending to oil-importing countries, that raised a further question of how to do it. The recycling could be managed either by the official sector—by governments and the IMF—or by the private sector. There was a choice to be made, in other words, between policymakers and markets. And, with some supportive elbowing from the U.S. government, markets won. Banks would take in deposits from newly rich oil exporters and lend that liquidity to the importers, whose financing needs had just spiked up.

With little debate, the proponents of an *officially* managed solution to the recycling problem were rather quickly silenced. One of these was Denis Healey, who had become Britain's chancellor of the exchequer in March 1974, a month after promising to squeeze the country's property speculators "until the pips squeak." Armed with a socialist's faith in the redistributive capacity of policymakers, Healey had proposed an official mechanism, a "comprehensive recycling scheme" through the IMF, that would funnel at least $25 billion of the OPEC surpluses to countries that had become saddled with deficits.

On the face of it, Healey's proposals were entirely consistent with the spirit of the postwar consensus on international capital flows. The Bretton

Woods regime that governed the international monetary system after 1945 put states and policymakers—not markets or currency traders—at the center of decision making about capital flows.

But Healey's instincts about the role that policymakers should play in this recycling process clashed heavily with the passionate preference for free-market capitalism that existed within President Nixon's Treasury Department. Reflecting on the U.S. response to his proposal for an official recycling mechanism, Healey wrote that "the Americans were bitterly opposed, because it would have meant interfering with the freedom of the financial markets—and with the freedom of the American commercial banks to make enormous profits out of lending to the Third World."[1] The American whose opposition counted particularly in this case was William Simon, the passionately pro-market U.S. treasury secretary, a "mean, nasty tough bond trader who took no BS from anyone," who was known to wake his children on weekend mornings with buckets of cold water.[2] Simon's view held sway.

Although some of the recycling of petrodollars was, in the end, intermediated through official facilities, it was really the bankers' moment. It wasn't just that the U.S. government was philosophically inclined to allow the private sector to manage the recycling process; it was also that the sheer size of financial markets was already dwarfing the resources available to policymakers. By the end of 1975, the combined assets of the twenty-one largest banks in the United States totaled nearly $400 billion. The lending resources of the IMF and the European Economic Community, by contrast, amounted to just over $20 billion.[3] Nor was it just a question of relative size but of relative confidence, too. The effective collapse of the Bretton Woods regime from 1971 had made it tough to have much faith in the capacity of governments to organize the world's monetary affairs. If governments couldn't manage it, the market was ready to step in.

Just as bankers had descended on Havana in the wake of the 1919 sugar boom, they found their way to Jeddah in 1974, only this time to source funds rather than to lend them. Among them was a thirty-seven-year-old David Mulford, then working for White Weld, a bank, but later to become the U.S. Treasury Department's under secretary for international affairs during the management of the crisis that would engulf the developing world in the 1980s. As he saw it, Saudi Arabia's sudden wealth "was simply mind blowing to investment bankers, aspiring entrepreneurs and con artists of every description."[4]

The task of mobilizing the funds that would finance the petrodollar recycling was actually rather straightforward. The Saudi Arabian Monetary Agency (SAMA), for example, was highly conservative in its investment philosophy. Untrusting of the international monetary system—not too surprising, given the turmoil that had followed Nixon's decision in the summer of 1971 to suspend the dollar's convertibility into gold—the Saudis expressed a strong preference for liquidity. That conservatism may well have been cemented by the fact that SAMA had been governed between 1958 and 1974 by Anwar Ali, a former staff member at the IMF, who, in the view of the *Financial Times* at least, committed the Saudis to "the most orthodox conventions of central banking practice."[5]

By the time Mulford was installed in Jeddah in late 1974, King Faisal had authorized only eighteen international banks to receive SAMA deposits. New banks could be added "only after the most careful scrutiny and the consent of the king and his council of ministers."[6] This preference for bank deposits in deciding how SAMA's dollars were kept was relaxed over time. But what remained consistent during the following years was *where* the dollars were kept. Between 1974 and 1982, Saudi Arabia's cumulative current account surplus was $160 billion, almost all of which was controlled by SAMA and almost all of which ended up in one place: the eurodollar market.[7]

The Supply of Credit

The ease with which petrodollars became a vehicle to finance the deficits of developing countries in the 1970s arose from the fact that these dollars flowed into a market that had been steadily built since the 1960s: the eurodollar market, a pool of dollar-denominated liquidity held in banks outside the United States, and overwhelmingly in London. By the time the oil crisis hit in 1973, the eurodollar market was a fully established financial infrastructure that could happily absorb the flow of petrodollars.

The eurodollar market was in some ways a child of the Cold War. Since state-owned banks in Eastern Europe liked to keep their export revenues out of the regulatory clutches of banks in New York, dollar deposits mushroomed in institutions such as Moscow Narodny Bank in London and Banque Commerciale pour L'Europe du Nord in Paris.[8] And the market's growth was assured because U.S.-based banks faced a raft of regulations that made it difficult for them to pay interest rates competitive enough to mobilize funds. The Fed's Regulation Q, for example, had set ceilings on interest rates offered by banks for deposits located in the United States. Holding deposits outside the United States allowed these banks to pay higher interest rates on their deposits, and had the additional advantage of allowing banks to avoid the U.S. interest equalization tax, which since 1963 had eaten into the returns on foreign securities held by U.S. residents. And by taking deposits outside the United States, banks could also avoid reserve requirements, so freeing up more resources to lend.

In other words, the growth of the eurodollar market was partly a story about international politics and partly a story about U.S. banks' efforts to escape financial repression at home. The net size of the market rose from $160 billion in 1973 to $600 billion by 1980.[9]

But the existence of petrodollars and the development of the eurodollar market don't offer a full explanation of what pushed credit toward developing countries in the 1970s. U.S. inflation also takes on a particular role in this story, largely because of what it did to the real, or inflation-adjusted, interest rate in the United States. At least until the late 1960s, the U.S. inflation rate had been unworryingly low, and so real interest rates were reliably positive. Throughout the 1960s, for example, U.S. inflation averaged 2.4 percent, and the average federal funds rate was 4.2 percent, giving a real interest rate of 1.8 percent. Since positive real interest rates act as a magnet for capital flows, this state of affairs kept money attracted to the United States.

By the early 1970s, though, the inflationary environment in the United States had changed beyond recognition because of three shocks. The first was a surge in agricultural prices that pushed U.S. food inflation up to 20 percent in 1973, from only 5 percent the year before. The second was the oil shock of October 1973, already described. And the third was the end, in April 1974, of a wage-price freeze that President Nixon had introduced in the summer of 1971.[10] Moreover, lurking behind these shocks was the dramatic depreciation of the dollar against other international currencies, a slide that had followed Nixon's suspension of the dollar's convertibility into gold in August of that year. By the summer of 1973, the dollar had lost a fifth of its value against other major currencies. Indeed, the diminishing purchasing power of OPEC's dollar-denominated revenues almost certainly helped convince OPEC to deploy the "oil weapon" in late 1973.

The U.S. inflation rate hit double digits in 1974, and would do so again in 1979–80 in the wake of the second oil shock. For the decade as a whole, the average U.S. inflation rate—around 7 percent—was almost three times the average of the previous two decades. And the result of this inflation was to push real U.S. interest rates below zero. The inflation-adjusted federal funds rate turned negative in 1974 and stayed negative through to 1980. The effect of this was to push capital toward developing countries in search of higher yields, just as negative real interest rates had pushed capital to Cuba in 1919.

And it seemed perfectly sensible for money to allow itself to be pushed toward developing countries, since this was the part of the world where growth prospects seemed brightest. Even before the oil shock, developing countries' GDP growth had started to exceed that of the industrialized world. This was a relatively new phenomenon, since even up to the mid-1960s it was normal to expect economic growth in the rich world to be faster than it was in the poorer one. Things had started to change in the late 1960s, though. Between 1968 and 1973—the era of Brazil's miracle—annual GDP growth in the developing world was an average of 7.5 percent, compared to 5.1 percent for industrialized countries as a whole. The growth differential, in other words, was 2.4 percentage points. By 1974, or year one of the petrodollar recycling process, the differential had risen to 5.2 percentage points: the developing world's growth rate was 6.1 percent, compared to a growth rate in the industrialized world of just 0.9 percent.

Banks were in the happy position of finding themselves trapped in a virtuous circle: negative real interest rates in the United States made it sensible to lend petrodollars to developing countries, which in any case looked attractive because of the more rapid economic growth rates to be found there. And since those loans would help support higher rates of investment spending in these countries, rapid growth in the developing world could be both the cause and the consequence of making petrodollars available to them. It helped, too, that since developing countries had effectively been locked out of world capital markets since the early 1930s, international banks weren't exactly overburdened with financial exposure to developing countries. On the contrary: banks had barely any exposure to them. New lending to these economies could be justified by the banks quite simply as a way of achieving a basic stock adjustment in their loan books, an exercise in portfolio diversification. And all this came with the enthusiastic encouragement of Washington. According to William Seidman, an economic adviser to President Gerald Ford, "The entire Ford administration, including me, told the large banks that the process of recycling petrodollars to the less developed countries was beneficial, and perhaps a patriotic duty."[11]

For banks, then, the economic incentives to lend to developing countries were clear. Finally, one innovation from the late 1960s made the wholesale mobilization of funds really quite simple: the syndicated rollover credit. Banks could lend in dollars at a margin over their cost of funds (the London Interbank Offered Rate, or LIBOR), which would be determined every three or six months on a floating basis. The risk of default by the borrower was spread across many banks by the loan manager responsible for putting together the syndicate of lending banks. The loan manager earned nice fees, and syndicate members could add assets to their balance sheets with minimal administrative cost. The banks carried neither interest rate risk nor currency risk: these belonged to the borrowers entirely.

The Demand for Credit

For developing countries, the idea of getting plentiful access to financing from international banks was a wholly new one in the postwar era. Before petrodollars existed, capital flows to developing countries were mostly made up of development aid and export credits offered by rich-country governments. Private capital flows were very much in the minority and were mostly accounted for by inflows of FDI. The legacy of bond defaults in the 1930s still lingered. In 1970, for example, the sum of export credits and official development assistance accounted for 60 percent of external financing for developing countries; FDI explained a further 20 percent.[12] Moreover, these flows were of tiny size in relation to the receiving countries' economies.

External financing from international banks—and what amounted to the privatization of capital flows to developing countries—opened up a world of pleasant possibilities for these economies. In the first place, the ability to borrow abroad allowed them to avoid the nasty alternatives of either adjusting to higher oil prices by squeezing their spending on imports of other goods or trying to do with less oil, either of which would have been recessionary. That would have been particularly unwelcome, since the rapid growth rates that developing countries had enjoyed in the late 1960s and early 1970s naturally generated popular expectations of more to come. The availability of external financing created a sense of hope that foreign capital could add to domestic savings, and so support levels of investment that would otherwise be unimaginable. This was the theme of a paper issued by the Brazilian central bank in 1973 titled "The External Sector and National Economic Development."[13] It reflected a line of thinking that was widespread at the time.

The ability to get funding from international banks had another attraction, too: it seemed to imply a much smaller loss of national sovereignty than any of the alternatives.

Inflows of FDI in particular had a bad smell in the early 1970s: allowing foreign firms to own manufacturing capacity seemed like an affront to a developing country's sense of autonomy. And this view was being strengthened by the growing role that foreign firms were playing in some places: by 1972, foreign-owned firms accounted for half of total manufacturing sales in Brazil.[14] One response to this sense of being taken over was to legislate: in 1973, for example, the Mexican government passed the "Law to Promote Mexican Investment and Regulate Foreign Investment," which had the effect of excluding foreign firms from investing in Mexican railways, electricity, or communications. In contrast, borrowing from international banks seemed to imply no compromise at all of national autonomy. This idea was nicely reinforced by the fact that banks seemed happy to lend without asking too many questions about how funds were to be spent. The petrodollar recycling process in the 1970s abandoned the principle that bank lending should be linked to some specific end use. Instead, lending was offered to support rising deficits in the budget and the balance of payments.

Trade deficits became as quickly visible for developing countries as the surpluses did for OPEC members. Between 1974 and 1977, major oil exporters enjoyed an aggregate current account surplus of $175 billion. Those countries included Algeria, Indonesia, Iran, Iraq, Kuwait, Libya, Nigeria, Oman, Qatar, Saudi Arabia, the UAE, and Venezuela. During the same period, the cumulative current account deficit of the rest of the developing world was around $145 billion. So the math of the recycling process was neat. And it is worth stressing how this really was a phenomenon associated with the developing world, not the developed one: during these years, the industrialized countries managed to eke out a total overall current account surplus of $6 billion.[15] Rich countries as a whole had little need for petrodollars: their main problem came from the inflationary consequences of the oil shock, rather than its effect on the balance of payments.

The logic of the petrodollar recycling process was that oil importers should, in effect, be borrowing the surpluses of oil exporters to finance their deficits. And at the start of the process in 1974 that is more or less what happened. The developing countries with the most obvious borrowing needs were oil-importing countries. But without much delay, oil-*exporting* countries also found themselves signing syndicated loan agreements and building up stocks of external debt.

In the end, a group of fifteen countries found themselves at the heart of the international lending boom of the 1970s: Argentina, Bolivia, Brazil, Chile, Colombia, Côte d'Ivoire, Ecuador, Mexico, Morocco, Nigeria, Peru, the Philippines, Uruguay, Venezuela, and Yugoslavia (the "Baker 15," described further in chapter 2). Since this group included oil exporters as well as oil importers, the obvious question is, what was common to these countries that made foreign borrowing so attractive?

The answer was simply the desire for growth. In the mid-1970s, it was perfectly reasonable for a developing country's policymakers to worry about economic performance: the industrialized world as a whole was perilously close to recession in 1974 and 1975, and the United States itself spent most of those two years suffering negative rates of GDP growth. Access to international financial markets allowed developing countries to supplement domestic savings with foreign savings and so keep their economies' engines running.

International borrowing was attractive for another reason, too: its ability to add muscle to the role of the state. The 1970s saw a vast spreading of the economic influence of the state in the developing world. This was enabled by access to credit, since governments had new resources with which to expand their sphere of activity. The number of Mexican state-owned enterprises, for example, grew from thirty-nine in 1970 to 1,155 in 1982; the government became not just an airline operator and hotel owner but a cheesemaker and sugar distributor.[16] Much of this expansion of the state was supported by the Mexican development bank, Nafinsa. As early as 1974, the bank held equity stakes in ninety-eight Mexican firms, and by the late 1970s Nafinsa was the obligor, or borrower, for around one-third of Mexico's external debt. In this state-centered world, Mexico's planning ministry, established in 1976, quickly became the most reliable path to ultimate power there: Miguel de la Madrid, Carlos Salinas de Gortari, and Ernesto Zedillo all held the position of planning minister before assuming the country's presidency.

The ability of governments to strengthen their role in the economy during the 1970s was made easier by the fact that they were largely doing the borrowing. In the 1970s, the private sector's external debt in the fifteen countries listed above rose from $15 billion to $63 billion. But the public sector's external debt, including guarantees issued on behalf of private sector borrowers, increased from $40 billion to $245 billion.

How ironic it is that the privatization of capital flows in the 1970s should coincide with a nationalization of economic power in the borrowing countries! Just when rich-country policymakers like Denis Healey seemed at risk of becoming slaves to market forces, policymakers in the developing world were able to feel like masters.

Nowhere was this rise of state power clearer than in Brazil. The country's external borrowing in the 1970s ushered in an era of "big projects," partly funded by generous subsidies available from the public development bank BNDES and from Banco do Brasil. These subsidies, and the rise of state-owned industrial enterprises in the energy, steel, telecommunications, and transportation sectors, would have been unthinkable without the resources available to the government from foreign borrowing. By 1978, public enterprises accounted for 78 percent of the assets of Brazil's 200 largest companies, up from 64 percent in 1972.[17]

Outside Latin America, too, external borrowing fed the growth of the state. The industrialization of Korea—which discovered the virtues of export-oriented development much sooner than did Latin America—was also very substantially state-driven. By the mid-1970s, the public sector was responsible for between a third and a half of investment in Korea.[18] The 1970s were a decade in which debt, industrialization, and the growth of the state each supported the other two.

Yet there were also countries where the growing strength of the state lived side by side with a more indulgent attitude toward the private sector and a more open attitude toward trade. Chile provided the perfect example of this approach. The coup that brought General Augusto Pinochet to power in September 1973 was publicly defended as a necessary response to the economic chaos that had been threatened by the socialism of his predecessor, Salvador Allende. And there was some good reason to describe Allende's economic policies as chaotic: in 1973, the budget deficit reached an astronomical 22 percent of GDP, a huge leap from previous years, and inflation exploded, hitting an average of 311 percent despite the existence of price controls.

Pinochet's efforts to achieve economic stabilization relied on tight fiscal and monetary policy. By 1975 the budget deficit was down to 2.5 percent of GDP. Yet the economic consequence of this dramatic fiscal squeeze was a severe contraction in the economy: GDP fell 13 percent in 1975. This was the age of the "Chicago Boys," U.S.-trained economists with a rigorous set of views fixated on minimizing the state's involvement in economic affairs and on liberating the private sector. Their influence, after Jorge Cauas took over the Finance Ministry in 1974, led to some revolutionary changes in the structure of the Chilean economy. Between 1974 and 1976, ninety-nine firms were privatized, along with thirteen packages of bank stocks, and the average import tariff fell from 94 percent to 27 percent.[19]

The decline in inflation took longer: it was only in 1977 that Chilean inflation fell back below 100 percent, having peaked at 750 percent in April 1974. It is in the inflation story where we see yet another source of the demand for credit on the part of borrowing countries. In the 1970s, developing-country policymakers discovered how capital inflows can help keep inflation low.

As Chile's experience shows, it wasn't only the United States or other rich countries that had to deal with inflation shocks in the 1970s. Inflation in developing countries had been relatively well behaved in the years running up to the 1973 commodity price shocks, remaining in the single digits on average in the late 1960s and early 1970s. But all that changed in 1973, just as it had for the United States, and by 1974 the average inflation rate for developing countries had risen to 21 percent. Although Chile's inflation rate for that year was exceptionally, even absurdly, high, there were plenty of other countries for which inflation was becoming an unwelcome distortion. In 1974 inflation reached 47 percent in Indonesia, 33 percent in the Philippines, and 28 percent in Turkey.

How could a developing country use capital inflows to push inflation down? The answer comes from the fact that capital inflows can help stabilize the nominal exchange rate. If a country keeps its exchange rate stable against the dollar while its inflation rate is high, then imports become cheaper relative to goods produced locally. That helps to push down the local inflation rate because the lower price of imported goods acts as a gravitational force on the price of goods in the whole economy. The consequence of making imported goods cheap is that the trade deficit widens, because more firms and households buy relatively inexpensive foreign goods. But when capital flows from abroad are available, that problem is solved because the deficit can be financed.

In other words, being able to borrow from abroad gave developing countries the chance to use exchange rates as a tool to push inflation down. So-called "exchange rate–based stabilization" made use of newly available capital flows to solve an inflation problem, just as these capital flows were simultaneously helping to support economic growth. Just as the breakdown of the Bretton Woods system of managed exchange rates was delivering a lesson to the developed world that fixing currencies was impossible, developing countries were discovering the opposite. The availability of external financing made it seem that pegging currencies, or heavily managing them, was rather straightforward.

The combination of relatively fixed exchange rates and relatively high domestic inflation in developing countries led, in plenty of cases, to a dramatic loss of competitiveness through an appreciation of the real, or inflation-adjusted, exchange rate. And in the 1970s that added a hugely destabilizing element to the relationship between developing countries and international finance. As dollars became extraordinarily cheap in real terms, the demand for them went up. And as this demand went up, capital *outflows* from developing countries became a more visible phenomenon, in the form of capital flight.

A Different Kind of Recycling

Capital flight is an idea that is tricky to pin down but implausible to deny. It is possible to question, for example, whether there was any real difference between an Argentine citizen who opened a bank account in Miami in, say, 1978 and an American who sold shares in IBM and bought shares in General Motors. Both the Argentine and the American could be described as "adjusting their portfolio." So the definition of "capital flight," as opposed to "portfolio reallocation," can be a matter of subjective judgment more than strict technical interpretation. But that value-laden distinction matters: the idea of capital "fleeing" a country seems to suggest that an investment is in conflict with the objectives of a country's policymakers, imposes some large economic cost on the country, or is in some sense illegal.

Capital flight in the late 1970s and early 1980s trapped developing countries in a vicious circle of needing to borrow further to finance these outflows. And sometimes the outflows weren't particularly visible: a popular form of expatriating capital is to lie about the value of trade. An exporter that wants to keep dollars abroad can simply understate the value of a shipment of goods that's being sold abroad, so that the difference between the shipment's true value and its reported value is kept offshore without detection.

As long as international borrowing was helping to sustain a state of affairs in which domestic residents could think that dollars were unsustainably cheap because of domestic currency overvaluation, those residents would keep buying them. And the countries that seemed to suffer the most dramatic capital flight were ones in which policymakers, in their pursuit of low inflation, allowed currencies to become overvalued and in which little effort was made to restrict capital outflows. Countries like Brazil or Korea, where exchange rate policy generally sought to avoid overvaluation, usually suffered less from capital flight.

For the countries that did suffer, its effects were devastating. In Argentina, for example, an exchange rate–based stabilization had initially helped to deliver an astounding appreciation of the inflation-adjusted exchange rate: if the level of the real exchange rate was 100 in 1975, by 1980 it had reached 270. This was achieved through the *tablita*, a pre-announced pace of currency devaluation much lower than the inflation rate. Argentines were dazzled by the purchasing power of their pesos and, given the ability to buy cheap dollars, began to take those dollars out of the country. These were the years of *plata dulce* ("easy money," loosely translated), when families of Argentines could be seen struggling through the airport in Buenos Aires on their way back from a shopping spree in Miami or Europe, laden with color TV sets.[20] The devastation here is the way in which an overvalued currency pushes up spending power abroad: middle-class Argentine consumers felt happy, but at the expense of draining the economy of foreign exchange.

In the 1980s, the question of how to measure capital flight became the subject of obtuse academic controversy, but an intuitive approach is to consider the sources and uses of foreign exchange. A country generates net inflows of foreign exchange from net foreign borrowing and from net inflows of FDI. It uses those sources to finance a current account deficit (if it has one) and to accumulate foreign exchange reserves. So one measure of capital flight is simply the difference between those sources and those uses. On this measure, two-thirds of the increase in Argentina's external debt between 1976 and 1982 can be explained by the need to finance capital flight. For Venezuela, almost *four-fifths* of its rise in indebtedness was necessitated by capital flight.[21]

The idea that developing countries were borrowing to finance capital flight caused banks some ambivalence. On the one hand, there was a slow accumulation of evidence that the flow of debt had become disconnected from investment spending, and that was a source of worry. If lending was no longer meaningfully supporting the economic development process, then the case for lending should, in theory, collapse. On the other hand, these same banks played a role in intermediating this flight and profited from it: their private banking operations were built up in these years to provide a home for the wealth that was seeping out of Latin America.

The birth of large-scale capital flight in the late 1970s grew into a phenomenon that would undermine the case for continued lending to developing countries, since the latter's accumulation of debt had clearly become unshackled from any activity that could generate a return sufficient to repay it. And from 1979 on, it wasn't just the acceleration of capital flight that threatened the sustainability of the banks' relationships with developing countries. There was also the small matter of the second oil shock and the response it elicited from the U.S. Federal Reserve.

The Descent

On February 1, 1979, a plane from Paris landed in Tehran with a passenger, Ayatollah Khomeini, whose arrival in Iran would lead to a second round of petrodollar recycling. The Iranian revolution that Khomeini led caused a collapse in the country's oil industry, with the result that during the first quarter of 1979 the world economy was operating with 2 million barrels per day less oil than it had in late 1978. By late 1979 the price of crude oil had reached $39 per barrel, having been below $13 per barrel during 1978. The increase was partly driven by the world's sense of panic that this new shock to the oil market was an echo of the dislocations that had accompanied the first shock six years earlier.

The second oil shock started a process that turned into a crisis three years later. International lending to developing countries continued because the established logic of petrodollar recycling demanded it. The combined current account surplus of the major oil-exporting countries, having fallen to just $3 billion in 1978, rose to $70 billion in 1979 and to $115 billion in 1980. So plenty of resources were available to finance a new recycling process, and banks remained willing. Indeed, the pace of international lending accelerated. In the six years between 1972 and 1978, banks had lent $130 billion to the fifteen major developing country borrowers, the "Baker 15." Yet in the three years between 1979 and 1981, banks lent $150 billion.

Banks were able to convince themselves that they were reliably managing the risks associated with the rising debt burden of sovereign borrowers in the developing world. Lending maturities grew shorter and lending spreads widened in the aftermath of 1979. Yet all this did was to produce a kind of collective-action problem: for any individual creditor, making new loans on less generous terms seemed like a simple act of prudence. Yet for creditors as a whole, the riskiness of their portfolios increased as the frequency and cost of refinancing for their sovereign borrowers became more and more burdensome.

Those risks were compounded by a pattern of behavior on the part of lenders that took on characteristics that were more animal than rational. The herd instinct is simply to do what others do, lend where others lend. This may seem irrational, but it doesn't lack reasons. The best way for a bank to make use of the information that it thinks others might have is to copy them. In the late 1970s and early 1980s, this was not self-evidently absurd, since this was a time when economic information about developing countries was relatively scarce, and published with long delays. Balance-of-payments data could take a year to materialize. The *World Bank Debt Tables* could be eighteen months out of date. So, for any individual lender, the information that was coming from what others were doing took on unusual significance. And since in any case a bank's performance is measured relative to that of its competitors, straying too far from what others are doing may not be sensible—particularly since it is usually more comfortable to be wrong in company than it is to be wrong on one's own. Moreover, following the herd can seem like a reasonable strategy because a country's creditworthiness is partly determined by its ability to borrow: as long as it can do so, then an argument, however circular, can be put together by any individual lender to keep lending.

The accelerated rise in the external debt stock of developing countries did tease out voices of dissent: economists and policymakers who worried about whether both borrowers and lenders were becoming irresponsible. Among these was Henry C. Wallich, a Federal Reserve Board member, whose concern was motivated by the principle that "credit is suspicion asleep." He made the point, in a 1981 speech, that by the end of 1980 there were eighty U.S. banks for which exposure to a single LDC amounted to over 30 percent of their capital, up from only thirty-six banks in June 1979. In some cases, he said, "one wonders whether for some banks their in-house country limits are not more nearly marketing objectives."[22]

Although the voices of concern about the risks facing developing countries grew louder from 1979, the banks remained confident. Walt Wriston, Citibank's chairman and the preeminent banker of his time, expressed that confidence aggressively in 1981: "It is no secret that over the years a lot of intellectual capital has been invested in the proposition that massive defaults in the Third World will cause a world financial crisis. Those who have taken this view since 1973–74 have been proved wrong, and those of us who believed the market would work proved correct."[23] And Wriston's was by no means a lone voice. The Group of Thirty, an informal think tank and economic consultative group, commissioned a survey in 1981 in which bankers were asked whether they saw any risk of a "generalized debt problem affecting developing countries." Seventy-two percent of the fifty-odd banks that took part in the survey said no.[24]

The truth is that there was no definitive piece of evidence in the late

1970s or the very early 1980s to suggest that a crisis was inevitable. One could hear complaints about the construction of shopping centers in Latin America that were unlikely to generate the foreign exchange needed to repay external debt, or complaints about "Pharaonic projects" in countries like Brazil.[25] But the memory of the mid-1970s was a reason to be cheerful: petrodollar recycling in its first incarnation certainly saved many countries from recession and gave international banks what looked like a healthy way of diversifying their loan portfolios.

This debate about the risk of a debt crisis in the developing world continued, more or less inconclusively, between 1979 and 1982. Building in the background, though, was the one factor destined to end the debate: U.S. monetary tightening.

The inflation shock of 1973 had pushed capital toward developing countries because the Fed's response to it had allowed real U.S. interest rates to turn negative. The inflation shock of 1979 did the opposite, however, because of the Fed's decisive efforts to kill inflation by ensuring that real U.S. interest rates became strongly positive. This process started almost as soon as Paul Volcker arrived at the Fed as chairman in August 1979: the first monetary tightening under his watch took place at the end of his first week in office and was followed by what became known as the "Saturday Night Special" in early October, when Volcker unveiled an entirely new approach to monetary policy, imposing constraints for the first time on the U.S. money supply.[26]

While the real federal funds rate had averaged close to minus 1 percent in the years between 1973 and 1979, its average rate between 1980 and 1982 was nearly plus 4 percent. Just as negative real U.S. interest rates had pushed capital toward developing countries, their sharp rise sucked it back. When the United States was ignoring its inflation problem in the 1970s, capital inflows helped developing countries solve *their* inflation problems by enabling them to prop up their exchange rates. But when the United States tried to solve *its* inflation problem, those capital flows to developing countries dried up.

U.S. monetary tightening tipped the developing world into crisis. It raised the cost of borrowing because of the LIBOR-linked structure of most commercial loans. It resulted in an appreciation of the dollar that altered the terms of trade for U.S. trading partners. And, critically, it helped to provoke a collapse in U.S. and global economic growth, destroying the capacity of developing countries to earn dollars through exports. The United States was in recession by early 1980, and after a brief recovery fell still more deeply into recession in 1982. Global GDP growth that year was 0.4 percent. Not until 2009, during the global financial crisis, would the world economy again face such a collapse in activity.

By 1982, both borrowers and lenders were in a state of deep distress. Interest and amortization payments on external debt absorbed 50 percent of export revenues that year for the fifteen most heavily indebted countries. And the banks found themselves almost absurdly exposed to these countries. By the end of 1982, the $54 billion of developing-country loans on the books of the eight largest U.S. banks accounted for 264 percent of their capital.[27]

Borrowers in the 1970s thought they had bought protection of their own sovereignty by taking in bank loans, because these were the flows that seemed the least compromising to national autonomy. And lenders thought that extending credit in dollars at floating interest rates gave them protection because they carried neither currency risk nor interest rate risk. Both borrowers and lenders were wrong. Floating-rate debt is fine when dollar interest rates are low. But what borrowers discovered when rates rose in the early 1980s is that U.S. monetary policy could exercise a kind of tyranny over their economic fate. It took almost a decade for the developing world to recover from the crisis that followed. And it would take almost a generation for developing countries to adapt themselves to a more fundamental problem: the overwhelming influence of the U.S. Federal Reserve in their economic life.

TWO

Exit Finance

Two Decades of Crisis

It is often the case that the "beginning of the crisis" isn't really the beginning of the crisis. For example, the financial shock that enveloped Asia in 1997 is usually dated from the devaluation of the Thai baht on July 2 of that year. But it was the devaluation of the Czech koruna in March that set the stage for what was to hit Asia a few months later. Likewise, the birthday of the "Tequila" crisis of the mid-1990s may not be December 20, 1994, when the Mexican peso was devalued after the central bank's foreign exchange reserves had evaporated, but sometime in the early months of that year, when the value of the Turkish lira fell by 50 percent. By the same token, the debt crisis of the so-called less developed countries (LDCs) in the 1980s may not really have been kicked off by Mexico's announcement on August 12, 1982, that it would suspend payments on its external debt. A better starting point is Poland, whose crisis in 1981 sent out an earlier signal that something was going very wrong in the relationship between developing countries and their creditors.

Cross-border bank lending to Poland had been supported by the "umbrella theory": if worst came to worst, the Soviet Union would shield Poland from default. This was a comforting idea to creditors since Poland wasn't,

39

at the time, a member of the IMF, and so it lacked a lender of last resort in Washington. By early 1981, though, the theory was proving itself wrong. A CIA analysis had concluded in February that Poland "can cover its hard currency obligations for only another two or three months,"[1] and by the end of March, the country was in debt restructuring negotiations with a committee of banks representing its 501 creditors. By then, four-fifths of the country's export revenues were being used to service its $25 billion of external debt. The government's first rescheduling agreement with its bank creditors was signed in September 1981, against a background of turbulence following hunger demonstrations that summer, provoked by widespread shortages of virtually everything. It wouldn't be the last.

Of course, there had been isolated debt restructurings during the 1970s—by Peru, Turkey, and Zaire, for example—but Poland's crisis was the first of an *era* of crises. It is conventional to think that these crises fell into two separate phases: the LDC debt crisis of the 1980s, which only properly ended in the early 1990s with debt write-offs and a loosening of U.S. monetary policy, and the emerging markets crises, which stretched from Turkey in 1994 through to the 2002 collapse of the Brazilian real. Nonetheless, it makes more sense to see these crises as a single tale of woe: their similarities are more instructive than their differences.

To get at this idea, let's consider the overall shape of the thirty-year period between the early 1970s and the early 2000s. In the 1970s, capital flows were pushed to developing countries for a number of reasons, but the central facts of the story were (1) an optimism about the growth prospects of a group of developing countries to which lenders had little financial exposure, (2) the availability of a new source of liquidity in the form of petrodollars, and (3) the way in which negative inflation-adjusted U.S. interest rates helped push that liquidity toward developing countries. In the 1980s, crisis erupted above all as a result of the financial chaos created when the U.S. Federal Reserve tightened monetary policy to curb inflation in the United States.

This pattern of events also stamped itself onto the 1990s. In the early part of that decade, U.S. monetary policy once again became a powerful force pushing capital toward developing countries. As the United States went into recession in early 1991, U.S. monetary policy eased sharply, with the result that by late 1992 the inflation-adjusted federal funds rate was once again negative, and it stayed exceptionally low throughout 1993—compared to an average real rate of 5.4 percent during the peak crisis years of 1981–85. And, as in the 1970s, a new source of liquidity, combined with this regime of exceptionally low interest rates, helped push capital to emerging markets. Instead of coming from petrodollar-funded U.S. banks, though, the new liquidity was an influx of cash from a new type of investor: the international asset management industry.

The flow of capital to developing countries in the early 1990s was exceptional: in 1993, the net inflow to all of them was around $200 billion, or something close to 4.5 percent of developing countries' GDP.[2] What was new about this flow is that it had relatively little to do with cross-border lending by commercial banks, which were still licking their wounds from the debt restructurings of the 1980s. Instead, the inflow of the early 1990s came from institutional investors in bonds, equities, and the local debt instruments of these countries. There was a naïve enthusiasm cheerleading these inflows that echoed the bushy-tailed optimism of the bankers twenty years previously. Lee Buchheit, a widely respected lawyer heavily involved in the restructuring of sovereign debt, described business class seats on airlines full of "eager young investment and commercial bankers clutching mandates for new Eurobonds, global depositary receipt issues, Euroconvertibles and so forth, or . . . mutual fund managers checking on the performance of their LDC investments."[3]

And just as the Fed's monetary tightening from 1979 had gradually squeezed cross-border lending to LDCs, a new round of tightening at the beginning of 1994 cut the supply of capital to emerging markets once again. Alan Greenspan, Fed chair since 1987, raised the federal funds rate in early February 1994 for the first time in five years to end what the Fed described as an "overly accommodative stance." Paul Sarbanes, a U.S. senator, nicely described this rate hike as a "bomber coming along and striking a farmhouse."[4] Directly inside the farmhouse were Turkey, whose exchange rate collapsed more or less immediately, and Mexico, for which the rate hikes of 1994 set the stage for an explosive crisis at the end of the year.

The Mexican crisis and its "Tequila" aftereffects, which delivered shocks to countries like Argentina and Hungary, didn't halt the flow of capital to emerging markets for long: by 1996, the year before Asia's financial crisis, net flows to emerging markets had risen to 5.6 percent of their GDP.[5] But just as the tightening of U.S. monetary policy had sucked capital from Turkey and Mexico in 1994, a different kind of tightening helped push Asia toward a crisis in 1997: not so much a rise in real U.S. interest rates (though the inflation-adjusted Fed funds rate did rise from 2 percent in late 1996 to 4 percent by the beginning of 1998) but a strengthening of the dollar. In early 1995 a dollar bought around 90 Japanese yen, but by early 1997 it had strengthened to 120 yen, delivering a nasty shock to the competitiveness of Asian exporters whose currencies were dollar-linked. This played a decisive role in triggering crises in Thailand, Indonesia, Korea, Malaysia, and the Philippines, and those crises, in turn, created links of contagion that generated crises in Russia (August 1998), Brazil (January 1999), Turkey (February 2001), and Argentina (December 2001). This chain of crises ended definitively only after a further collapse in the Brazilian real from March 2002.

The point of this potted history is to identify a single theme that runs through three decades of the relationship between developing countries and international finance, between the early 1970s and the early 2000s. That theme is, in essence, the boom-and-bust cycle of capital flows, and the role that U.S. monetary conditions played in the timing of the booms and the busts. The task of this chapter is to identify more precisely the features that help explain these decades as one extended episode, connected by a number of similarities. Before we get to that, though, a word about the differences.

As we saw in chapter 1, capital flows to LDCs in the 1970s were characterized by a particular type of creditor (banks) lending to a particular type of debtor (governments), with a particular type of instrument (syndicated loans) priced in a particular way (at floating rates), denominated in a particular currency (dollars), within a particular economic climate (the growth of the state's role in supporting development), and with a particular set of consequences (a long, painful economic crisis in the 1980s).

By the 1990s, things had changed. Bondholders, equity investors, and foreign direct investors replaced banks (though Asia was different, as we shall see); private sector borrowers replaced public sector ones; borrowing at fixed interest rates replaced borrowing at floating rates; the private sector replaced the public sector as the desirable engine of growth; and crises proved shorter-lived.

La Década Perdida

Set against subsequent developments, it is the lengthy duration of the 1980s crises that deserves attention. The 1980s were universally characterized as a "lost decade" for Latin America in particular, after Mexico followed in Poland's footsteps and suspended debt payments in August 1982. In 1980, Latin America's per capita GDP was almost 40 percent of the average in advanced economies; by 1990 it had fallen to 28 percent.

To understand why the crises in the 1980s lasted so long, two factors above all will help. The first is the cloudiness of the distinction between a country that has a liquidity problem (where it is simply running out of cash) and one that has a solvency problem (where the debt stock is unpayable). The second is the high cost of addressing a solvency problem.

In the early years of the 1980s crises, developing countries were almost universally considered to be merely illiquid, a problem capable of being addressed through a three-pronged strategy coordinated in Washington. First, banks would agree to reschedule countries' maturing principal repayments (and how: by the end of 1982, twenty-seven countries were negotiating with their creditors). Second, banks would further agree to inject new money into debtor countries to help them refinance interest payments coming due. Third, the IMF (along with other official lenders, such as the World Bank and the Inter-American Development Bank) would support countries with lending of its own as long as the debtors pursued policies that restricted their financing needs in an effort to stabilize the balance of payments. This was essentially a "Bagehotesque" approach, applying Walter Bagehot's analysis of 1873 that "a panic, in a word, is a species of neuralgia, and according to the rules of science you must not starve it."[6] Managing a panic according to this principle required the relevant institution to lend to stricken borrowers "whenever the security is good": exchanging funds for collateral, in other words.

The collateral, in this case, took the shape of conditionality attached to IMF lending, rather than real or financial assets. The IMF took on the responsibility of ensuring that developing countries, on the receiving end of the benefits of rescheduled principal payments and (involuntary) new money from banks, were tightening fiscal and monetary policy in an effort to limit their need for external financing—and so to help generate a positive net supply of dollars, now that international banks could no longer be relied on to keep on lending to them. Just as conventional collateral—such as a pledge of assets—protects creditors from losses, the IMF's conditionality sought to protect creditors by ensuring that borrowers became net generators of foreign exchange.

One way of capturing the effects of all this is through the idea of a "net resource transfer," which measures the total flow of dollars to a developing country from net cross-border lending and FDI, less interest and dividend payments. During the seven years between 1976 and 1982, the fourteen biggest developing country debtors enjoyed a total positive net resource transfer of some $83 billion. During the following seven years, between 1983 and 1989, that resource transfer turned negative—that is, it became an outflow—to the tune of $134 billion. This is, in dollar terms, what a "lost decade" looks like: foreign exchange drained out of Latin America and out of a number of countries in other regions. With no available external financing, spending on imports collapsed, with the result that the aggregate current account deficit of these countries, some $50 billion in 1981, had turned into a surplus of $1 billion by 1985.

Defining the 1980s crises as ones of liquidity was a matter of survival as far as the banks were concerned. The reason for this was that the U.S. banks had, as we saw at the end of the previous chapter, a level of exposure to developing countries that would have proved ruinous if any alternative analysis had prevailed. If the crises had been described as one of insolvency, that would have implied the need for developing countries' debt to be at least partially written off. And since those write-offs would have effectively decapitalized the U.S. banks, any discussion of insolvency in the early 1980s had to end before it began. U.S. bank regulators were thus meticulous in ensuring that banks did not, in the early days of crisis, need to create loan-loss provisions against their exposure. William Seidman, Gerald Ford's economic adviser, put it this way: "U.S. bank regulators, given the choice between creating panic in the banking system or going easy on requiring our banks to set aside reserve for Latin American debt, had chosen the latter course. It would appear that the regulators made the right choice."[7]

A punchier view was expressed by Karin Lissakers, who later became the U.S. representative on the executive board of the IMF: "Perhaps not since the days of gunboat diplomacy has a U.S. government so carefully tailored public policy to suit the interests of large private banks."[8]

At the heart of this distinction between liquidity and insolvency during the 1980s was the ability of the banks to argue that debtor countries that had borrowed irresponsibly could squeeze their spending further to generate the liquid foreign exchange needed to repay the perfectly legal claims held by creditors. At the absurd extreme of this idea was Romania, whose president, Nicolae Ceauşescu, announced in April 1989 that the country had repaid its entire $10 billion external debt. What Ceauşescu described as the "outstanding result of our people's work" was a traumatizing Stalinist austerity drive that deprived Romanians of heating in subzero temperatures and of the basics of life in almost every respect.[9]

If Ceauşescu had been more patient, Romania would very likely have benefited from write-offs by creditors after all. The reason is that the analysis of the 1980s crises slowly metamorphosed from one of illiquidity to one of insolvency, with the inevitable consequence that debts were canceled. That this should be the case was well captured by Paul Volcker: "I'm not sure I've ever seen a pure liquidity problem. Typically, significant liquidity problems arise because there is some question of solvency, or there would be no lack of willing lenders. Put plain, if your credit is unassailable, you can nearly always raise money and stay afloat."[10]

This evolution in the way the crises of the 1980s were understood depended on two things. The first was the failure of developing countries to show any signs of being able to grow their way out of debt. The second was the increasing ability of the banks, in the latter part of the decade, to *afford* to write off debt.

By 1985, the strength of the U.S. dollar and the weakness of global commodity prices had caused a new round of gloom to set in about developing countries' growth prospects. The result of this was the formulation of a new strategy to deal with the debt crisis: the Baker Plan, named after the new U.S. treasury secretary James Baker and unveiled in October of that year at the annual meetings of the IMF and World Bank in Seoul. The initiative called for banks to lend an additional $20 billion, around 3 percent of their exposure, over the three-year period from 1986 to 1988 to fifteen large developing countries (the "Baker 15"). Multilateral development banks—the World Bank and the Inter-American Development Bank, for example—would also increase their lending by around $9 billion over three years. In exchange, developing countries themselves would commit to sustaining fiscal adjustment and to implementing structural economic reforms consisting of import liberalization, removal of restrictions on inflows of foreign investment, and privatization.[11] The objective, though it turned out to be excessively hopeful, was that these policies would push indebted countries onto a new path that would allow them to reduce their debt burdens by virtue of economic growth alone.

The Baker Plan failed in terms of its own objectives, even though it succeeded in one respect. The lending targets it set out weren't met: commercial banks and the multilateral development banks both fell short of the lending commitments in the plan, while the IMF was actually taking net repayments from the fifteen countries during this period.[12] The plan also failed in the sense that there was no evidence of a spurt in growth that could have made the fifteen countries' debts payable. But it succeeded in that it helped to buy time for the banks to get to a position in which they could afford to acknowledge the consequence of thinking that there was a solvency problem in the developing world: that consequence was the debt write-offs that formed the core of the Brady Plan, introduced in 1989.

The catalyst that allowed a solvency problem to be broadly acknowledged was the announcement by Citibank on May 19, 1987, that it had built a $3 billion loan-loss reserve against its exposure to developing countries, a sum equal to around 30 percent of its entire exposure to LDCs. As Citibank's then chair, John Reed, explained, "We don't see anything in the global economy that will allow these countries to get out of these problems soon."[13] Other lenders quickly copied this initiative, and as a result, the banks' unprotected exposure to stricken debtors fell sharply. In 1981 the $54 billion of LDC loans on the books of the eight "money center" banks in the United States amounted to 232 percent of the sum of their capital and reserves. By the end of 1987, in the wake of the buildup of the loan-loss reserves, that exposure was down to 125 percent of their loss-absorbing capacity.[14] Having acknowledged, through the creation of the reserves, that a portion of LDC debt was effectively unpayable, banks could now afford to cut the nominal value of the debt owed to them, passing the benefits of its unpayability to the borrowers.

At the heart of the Brady Plan—named after Nicholas Brady, President Ronald Reagan's last treasury secretary—was David Mulford, whose career had progressed from Jeddah to Washington, where he had become under secretary for international affairs at the U.S. Treasury. In essence, the plan was a kind of triangular arrangement between banks, debtors, and the IMF. Banks agreed to exchange their loans to a debtor country for new bonds, with the bonds having a face value of, say, 65 percent of the original claim. The banks were more or less happy to do this because the principal of the new bonds (together with some of the interest payments) was fully guaranteed by a zero-coupon U.S. Treasury bond purchased by the debtor country with funds made available to it by the IMF. The conversion of commercial bank debts into tradable securities fit comfortably with developments taking place in global capital markets. Indeed, the banks' loans to developing countries had been trading in an increasingly vibrant secondary market since the mid-1980s, and the discounts at which debts traded helped nudge the world toward an acknowledgment that these loans were not worth their face value.

By 1994, Brady deals had been extended to eighteen countries, covering a face value of just under $200 billion worth of debt. With a cute symmetry, one of the very last countries to crystallize debt relief under the Brady Plan that year was Poland: the first country into the debt crisis was pretty much the last out of it.

"Collateralized debt reduction," a more formal description of the Brady Plan, was widely praised as the panacea that lifted developing countries from their 1980s debt crises and allowed them to regain access to international financial markets in the early 1990s. And in truth, it is perfectly plausible to claim that an improvement in a country's external balance sheet—the difference between its foreign liabilities and its foreign assets—can help inject international confidence.

But while the Brady Plan was delivering improvements to the balance sheets of developing countries in the early 1990s, other forces were shaping up to give them renewed access to international finance. These were precisely the forces that had helped push capital to developing countries in the 1970s: loose U.S. monetary policy, new sources of liquidity, and optimism about growth in the developing world. A closer look across the period from the early 1970s to the early 2000s will help develop the idea that the booms and busts in capital flows to developing countries during this period were defined by a number of common features.

The Fed Gave, and the Fed Hath Taken Away

Having played a decisive role in pushing capital toward developing countries in the 1970s, U.S. monetary policy in the early 1990s once again helped money find a home outside the United States. The federal funds rate had remained above 9 percent on average during 1989, the year the Brady Plan was launched. But by the end of 1993 the rate was 3 percent. So, even if the Brady Plan had never existed, developing countries would have enjoyed a decent amount of cash flow relief as U.S. interest rates fell. On the $60 billion debt that Mexico owed to international banks at the end of 1988, for example, a 600-basis-point fall in the fed funds rate would save the country over $3.5 billion per year, equivalent to a not inconsiderable 1 percent of GDP.

The loosening of U.S. monetary policy in the early 1990s had a kind of twin effect on capital flows to developing countries. First, it increased the opportunity cost of keeping funds in the United States, or, put another way, it increased the incentive for investors to seek higher-yielding investments abroad. Second, it helped improve the apparent creditworthiness of the countries themselves by easing their debt-servicing burden.

Moreover, the effect of falling real U.S. rates in the early 1990s was more powerful than it had been in the early 1970s, for a couple of reasons. For one, the global integration of capital markets meant that that there was simply more money around that could turn on its heels in response to any change in U.S. monetary conditions. In the early 1970s, the stock of international assets on the aggregate balance sheet of the developed world was equivalent to less than 30 percent of its GDP. By the early 1990s, that stock exceeded 60 percent of GDP.[15]

At the same time, capital account liberalization was making developing countries more open to foreign money. Country after country reduced barriers to international capital inflows in the late 1980s and early 1990s. And why not? After the tribulations of the 1980s debt crises, the apparent willingness of international finance to return to developing countries must have felt like the spring sunshine. Policymakers in the developing world were naturally inclined to let that sunshine in, not least because of the official encouragement for this that was coming from Washington. As the IMF itself later acknowledged, the fund "did not hesitate" to support capital account liberalization in the early 1990s.[16] If the loosening of U.S. monetary policy was pushing capital toward developing countries, the opening of their capital accounts was pulling it, too.

One country that had completed the process of capital account liberalization by the late 1980s was Turkey.[17] This new openness to external financing seemed safe: it wasn't the government that was borrowing directly from international markets but Turkish banks. Yet what was actually being financed during this boom in capital flows was an explosion in government spending: public sector wages doubled in the late 1980s and early 1990s, an increase far higher than the rate of inflation, and the Turkish government extended itself further with generous agricultural support policies and spending on public enterprises. This populism reached a kind of peak with the election of Tansu Çiller as prime minister in June 1993. As a result, Turkey's growth model was pushed toward a reliance on domestic spending rather than exports, and this helped draw imports into the country. Inevitably, the trade gap widened: while Turkey had had a current account surplus of 0.7 percent of GDP in 1989, this had turned into a deficit of almost 3 percent of GDP by 1993.

In Mexico, another country that had enthusiastically opened its capital account in the early 1990s, the government was emphatically not at the root of the widening of the trade deficit during the early 1990s. Fiscal policy in Mexico during this period was a paragon of virtue: the stock of Mexico's public domestic debt fell from 20 percent of GDP in 1989 to 12 percent in 1992. But the deterioration in Mexico's balance of payments was more spectacular and more sustained than was the case in Turkey. By 1994, Mexico's current account deficit was 5.6 percent of GDP, double what it had been at the start of the decade.

So, what was driven by a spending spree in the public sector in Turkey in the early 1990s was driven by a spree in the private sector in Mexico. But both countries witnessed a phenomenon that had been well established in the 1970s and 1980s: namely, the fate of a country's current account—indeed, the fate of its economy as a whole—is intimately tied to the availability of external financing. When inflows exist, imports can be financed, and so they will be, allowing the economy to be kept afloat. In a sense, then, what happens to the capital account of the balance of payments can *cause* a change in the current account. And because that is the case, when capital inflows go into reverse, it becomes impossible to keep financing the current account deficit. What lies behind the reduction of a current account deficit when capital disappears is a decline in imports. And what lies behind the decline in imports is a decline in spending in the economy. Turkey's GDP contracted by 5.5 percent in 1994, Mexico's by 5.8 percent in 1995.

And for both countries in 1994, the trigger for that change in the availability of external financing was precisely what it had been in the early 1980s: a nasty shock from the Fed. As we saw earlier, the Fed's decision in February 1994 to tighten monetary policy for the first time in five years had the effect of dropping a bomb on emerging economies that had benefited from capital inflows encouraged by loose U.S. monetary conditions. The shock was particularly visible at the longer end of the U.S. yield curve. The yield on the ten-year U.S. government bond had fallen from 9 percent in 1990 to just above 5 percent in late 1993. By November 1994 the yield was back above 8 percent. And in an age in which bond markets had assumed the prominence that commercial banks had had twenty years earlier, the sort of damage done by increases in LIBOR in the early 1980s was better measured in the early 1990s by increases in bond yields.

This "tyranny" of U.S. monetary policy can also be understood in another way. A developing country whose exchange rate is pegged to the dollar will gain or lose competitiveness to the extent that the dollar is weakening or strengthening. It wasn't just Asia's crises that were triggered by the dollar's rise in the mid-1990s. A sharp appreciation of the dollar in 2000 and 2001 helped set the stage for crises in Turkey and Argentina. So the best way to think about developing countries' sensitivity to U.S. monetary policy isn't just through the effect of changes in the real interest rate of the dollar; it is also through changes in the dollar itself.

There is an underlying equation at work in emerging markets crises: *crisis = vulnerability + trigger*. The kind of shock a market receives when bad things happen has a lot to do with its underlying resilience. The most dangerous trigger during these crisis decades was a change in U.S. monetary conditions. But none of this gives us much of an answer to the obvious question: what defines vulnerability?

"This Time Is Different"

"The essence of the this-time-is-different syndrome is simple. It is rooted in the firmly held belief that financial crises are things that happen to other people in other countries at other times; crises do not happen to us, here and now."[18] This description by Carmen Reinhart and Kenneth Rogoff neatly captures a theme that links the surge in capital flows to developing countries in the 1970s with that of the 1990s. In both periods, the accumulation of debt was built on an assumption that the superior growth prospects of the developing world would inevitably generate the returns needed to repay ever-growing stocks of debt. That assumption was hubristic.

Neither borrowers nor lenders can claim any monopoly on hubristic thinking. Reflecting on Mexico's borrowing in the 1970s, Ángel Gurría, a man at the heart of Mexican policymaking for decades from the early 1980s, said it simply enough: "We overborrowed, yes. Why? Because we were not prudent enough. Because we thought things were going to stay the same forever."[19]

And just as the expectation of rapid growth fueled the accumulation of debt in the 1970s, a new surge of optimism lay at the center of the boom in capital flows that started in the early 1990s. That optimism was reinforced by the sense that the state-centric development models that developing countries had adopted with such enthusiasm in the 1970s were being ditched in favor of market-oriented economic reforms implemented by a new generation of policymakers. This helped seal the idea that the horrific legacy of the 1980s debt crises made it somehow inconceivable that similar crises could revisit the developing world any time soon. Commenting on that decade, Paul Volcker concluded that "for all the pain, the implications were not entirely negative. . . . The agony of the debt crisis provided the jolt necessary for Latin American leaders to rethink their old approaches and set off in fresh and much more promising directions."[20]

The adoption of what might be characterized as "Victorian virtue" in economic policy—through prudent trade liberalization, privatization, discipline over public finances, and the pegging of exchange rates to maintain local price discipline—seemed to guarantee economic liftoff. Some of the countries that seemed to live these virtues most observantly were rewarded with the ultimate accolade of membership of the Organization for Economic Cooperation and Development (OECD), often described as the club of rich nations. As an almost perfect illustration of what hubris can do, however, OECD membership became better described as the OECD curse. Mexico's entry in May 1994 preceded its crisis by six months; the Czech Republic joined in December 1995 and suffered a devaluation of the koruna fifteen months later; and Korea's accession in December 1996 occurred less than a year before the won's collapse in late 1997.

In the early 1990s, this idea that developing countries had turned a corner was powerfully reinforced by the emergence of new kinds of external financing, in much larger amounts than had previously been seen. The most encouraging evidence came from the appearance of larger flows of FDI, a form of capital that helped solidify the links between developing countries and the global economy. In the late 1970s and 1980s, FDI inflows weren't quite invisible, but they were certainly small, equivalent to no more than half a percent of developing countries' GDP in any year. By the early 1990s, though, FDI flows to emerging economies had reached almost 2 percent of their GDP. And the new role played by institutional investors, buying bonds and equities in emerging markets, helped sell the idea that we were in a new, globalizing world. By 1993, "emerging markets funds" were being advertised on U.S. television and in popular magazines, their rise more or less precisely echoing the growth of "coupon-clipping" households in the 1920s.[21]

The mere fact that external financing becomes available for a country helps fuel a sense of confidence. As capital flows in, a country will begin to look more creditworthy in the eyes of investors: after all, one of the features of a creditworthy borrower is simply its ability to borrow. So a surge in capital flows, by raising expectations of creditworthiness, begets more capital inflows. The process is circular, and that circularity creates vulnerability by encouraging both creditors and debtors to dull their sensitivity to risk.

And it is the *expectation* of accelerating income growth, rather than any evidence of it, that is the most powerful driver of the sense that "this time is different." Russia, for example, was locked into what seemed to be a permanent recession in the early and mid-1990s, thanks to an astonishing collapse in investment spending that followed the dissolution of the Soviet Union: real per capita GDP fell by a quarter between 1992 and 1998. However, that didn't stop Russia becoming a darling of international investors in the mid-1990s. Their enthusiasm was shaped by the emergence of energetic young reformers in government, the apparent triumph of liberal values, and the thought that Russia was "too big, too nuclear" to fail. Much the same thing happened in Mexico. The early 1990s saw a big improvement in Mexico's commitment to economic reform and a visible rise in the strength of the country's balance sheet as the public debt burden fell. But growth was elusive: per capita GDP growth was a grim 2 percent in the early 1990s.

Nowhere was the assumption that this time is different more clearly at the root of the crisis than in Asia during the 1990s. Korea, Thailand, Indonesia, and Malaysia had indeed enjoyed transformations that could fairly be described as economic miracles. From the early 1970s to the mid-1990s, average GDP growth rates for these countries had ranged from 6.9 percent in Indonesia to 8.4 percent in Korea. These growth rates had spectacularly delivered the region from economic misery: while six out of ten East Asians had lived in absolute poverty in 1975, that number had fallen to two out of ten by the mid-1990s.[22]

And that growth was based on three features that seemed highly attractive to international investors. One was Asia's export-oriented economic model: the stronger a country's export-generating capacity, the stronger its ability to repay debts denominated in foreign currencies. A second was the fact that Asian economies had—historically at least—kept their exchange rates competitive, avoiding the kind of disorienting overvaluations seen in Latin America during the 1970s. A third was the region's high savings ratios. The more a country can rely on its own savings to finance its domestic investment needs, the less it needs to rely on external financing. And on the principle that a bank prefers to lend money to a borrower who doesn't need to borrow, these high savings ratios were a particularly desirable feature of the Asian growth model for international investors.

All this helped attract substantial flows of capital to Indonesia, Korea, Malaysia, the Philippines, and Thailand. Between 1991 and 1996, net private capital inflows to these five countries grew to almost absurd proportions. On average, the net inflow of foreign capital into these countries rose from around 5 percent of GDP in 1992 to 10 percent of GDP in 1996. The scale of these capital inflows was greater than anything Latin America had seen in the 1970s, and greater than anything Mexico had seen during the boom in capital flows that preceded its December 1994 devaluation of the peso.

But in one critical sense, nothing at all was different in Asia. Just as in the 1970s for Latin America, the capital inflows reaching Asia during the 1990s came largely from international banks. In the three years leading up to Asia's crisis, from 1994 to 1996, commercial banks accounted for around half of the total net inflow of foreign funding. Just as Latin American countries learned in the 1980s that banks can be fickle creditors, so Asia was to learn the same in 1997. And the inflows from international banks were motivated above all by the lure of Asia's pegged exchange rates.

Stable Currency, Stable Country

"I will defend the peso like a dog." With these words the Mexican president José López Portillo expressed, in the summer of 1982, what many national leaders have thought or said in different words in the period between the early 1970s and the late 1990s: the credibility of a government is indexed by the stability of its currency. Indeed, the stability of the currency at the end of López Portillo's administration—his successor, Miguel de la Madrid, took over on December 1, 1982—was such an overwhelming priority that restrictions on the peso's convertibility were imposed in a last-ditch effort to protect it. It was a slightly absurd solution: we may not let you buy dollars, but at least they will remain reasonably priced!

Similar desperation measures aimed at maintaining currency stability were launched in Thailand in May 1997, for example, when the government restricted the ability of residents to buy dollars, and in Argentina in 2001, when the *corralito*, a measure to limit access to bank accounts, was introduced. In each of these cases, and in many more, the scale of capital outflows was overwhelming: expressing a commitment to defend a currency isn't the same as being able to do so. When a central bank's holdings of dollars are depleted and when it is unable to raise interest rates indefinitely to preserve the attractiveness of the currency, the authorities quickly run out of options. The Mexican peso's 1982 collapse followed on December 19, the Thai baht's on July 2, 1997, and Argentina's one-to-one peg with the dollar ended in early January 2002—in other words, shortly after policies to preserve currency stability had been introduced in all three cases. López Portillo's promise is enshrined in the name popularly given to his house in Mexico City, *La Colina del Perro*, Dog's Hill.

The allure of a fixed, or heavily controlled, exchange rate was pervasive across the developing world during these years. The IMF was able to claim that in 1991 almost four-fifths of emerging economies had exchange rates that were either fully pegged or heavily managed, the latter kept within a formal or informal band that limited their ability to fluctuate.[23]

Why were managed exchange rates so attractive to developing countries during these years? There are three explanations. One derives from the logic of political credibility already hinted at: since a volatile currency can be interpreted as some kind of proxy for economic or institutional weakness, it is easy to see how a policymaker might prefer a fixed exchange rate in the sense that it communicates a message of stability about the country as a whole, and hence about the credibility of the policymaker. Another explanation has to do with the contribution that a stable exchange rate can make to the predictability of a country's economic environment: if economic agents don't have to worry about currency volatility, that (in principle) might help tboost investment by encouraging "animal spirits."

A third and more technical justification for pegged or managed exchange rates lies in the role they can play in controlling inflation: through exchange rate–based stabilization, or ERBS, similar to Argentina's *tablita* of the late 1970s and described in the previous chapter. By pegging a currency to the dollar, a central bank is loosely subcontracting its monetary policy to the Fed. And importing the credibility of U.S. monetary policy into the domestic economy can help to push inflation down.

These stabilization strategies were very common throughout the thirty-year period from the late 1970s: considerably more than fifty episodes can be identified during this period.[24] And to repeat the point made in chapter 1: ERBS regimes really become attractive when capital flows are available. If a country's inflation rate is running higher than those of its trading partners, a currency peg will pretty much guarantee that the real, or inflation-adjusted, exchange rate becomes less competitive. That, in turn, tends to widen the trade and current account deficits—because imports become cheaper in terms of the local currency—and that requires external financing. It is no coincidence, then, that the popularity of ERBS coincided with an era in which developing countries gained access to international capital markets.

Yet the combination of fixed exchange rates and internationally mobile capital proved to be toxic. In a country with relatively high inflation, domestic interest rates will, naturally enough, be relatively high too. But the openness of the capital account makes those high interest rates available to international investors, and the capital inflows that result increasingly take on the characteristics of highly mobile "hot money," with the risk that a country's reserves can be easily exhausted when a trigger causes that money to reverse direction.

An example is Russia, in the buildup to its August 1998 crisis. In 1997, investors' enthusiasm for Russia was at its peak: Boris Yeltsin had success-fully fended off a challenge for the presidency in the summer of 1996 by the Communist Party candidate Gennady Zyuganov, the country's Western orientation seemed entrenched, and the government had the backing of a $10 billion IMF program. By early 1998, foreigners owned close to $20 billion in short-term Russian treasury bills, or GKOs, whose average yield during the course of 1997 had been over 26 percent. Since the ruble was effectively pegged to the dollar, that yield was also approximately the yield available to investors in dollars—in a year when an equivalent U.S. govern-ment Treasury bill would generate a return of just above 5 percent.

Examples like this abounded in the 1990s and at the start of the 2000s. In Turkey, during 2000, the predictability of the lira—that is, before it became unpredictable following its collapse on February 22, 2001—meant that the average yield in dollars available from owning a lira-denominated Treasury bill was close to 34 percent. Interest rates available in precrisis Asia were less eye-watering than this, but the effect was the same: vulnerability rose because short-term capital flows were sucked in by too-good-to-be-true yields in developing countries.

The bias in favor of short-term cross-border lending in the 1990s was also sewn into the regulatory fabric of international finance. "Basel I" was a framework for minimum capital requirements for banks, published by the Basel Committee on Banking Supervision in the wake of the 1980s crises with the aim of linking banks' capital adequacy to the riskiness of their lending. The overall objective was to ensure that banks kept capital at least equal to 8 percent of their risk-adjusted assets as a loss-absorbing buffer. While that was a noble enough objective, Basel I's system for risk-adjusted lending to emerging economies had the effect of giving banks an incentive to lend at maturities of less than one year: long-term loans to non-OECD countries carried a 100 percent weight in banks' calculations of their assets, but short-term loans carried only a 20 percent weight. It became cheaper, in other words, for banks to supply short-term—and ultimately more volatile—cross-border financing.[25]

Yet it is surprisingly difficult to be precise about the nature of market vulnerability. We've seen how relatively high inflation rates in developing countries can cause competitiveness to disappear when the exchange rate is more or less pegged to the dollar: local prices are rising, but the exchange rate's stasis means that the currency's international value is not weakening to offset those price increases. So one aspect of vulnerability is the appreciation of the real exchange rate, creating a form of *plata dulce* in which dollars become so cheap in terms of the local currency that some kind of problem will end up being created: either growth will collapse because domestic goods and services are too expensive or the current account deficit—shorthand for the country's external financing needs—will grow to a point where foreign lenders have had enough.

Argentina's experience in the 1990s helps illustrate this. Argentina's exchange rate peg took the form of a legal obligation on the part of the central bank to exchange one peso for one dollar. That obligation had been enshrined in the 1991 "convertibility law" created by Domingo Cavallo, President Carlos Menem's energetic economy minister, and was a self-conscious attempt to refer back to Argentina's golden years during the globalization era of the early twentieth century: a similar convertibility regime had underpinned Argentina's economic success in the years running up to the global collapse of the 1930s. The idea behind this regime was that a "hard" peg, rooted de jure in legislation, would be considerably more unbudgeable than a "soft," de facto peg rooted only in the intentions of policymakers.

And so it seemed to prove. As an ERBS mechanism, the convertibility regime was spectacularly successful: an inflation rate that had reached 20,000 percent in early 1990 was in single digits by late 1993. The government's commitment to the convertibility regime seemed rock-solid and was backed up by a sustained effort to introduce the kind of reforms that had been embodied in the Washington Consensus: an abolition of price controls, a reduction of tariffs, an openness to foreign capital, and privatizations of the companies supplying telecoms, electricity, gas, water, transport, hotel lodging, and air travel. Although Argentina suffered a recession in 1995 in the wake of the Mexican crisis, it gained the support of a precautionary IMF lending facility the following year that stamped Washington's seal of approval on the convertibility regime.

Argentine inflation seemed to have been tamed, but the persistence of even relatively low inflation rates meant that the currency became progressively more expensive in real terms: between 1990 and 2001, the inflation-adjusted, trade-weighted exchange rate of the Argentine peso strengthened by 90 percent. In turn, this meant the economy produced apparently endless current account deficits that needed external financing.

Those deficits remained intact even when, in the wake of the Asian crisis, Argentina fell once again into recession at the end of 1998. That was a particularly worrying sign for international investors: a recession can usually be expected to get rid of a current account deficit because the collapse in domestic spending helps cut the import bill. But that won't happen if dollars remain too cheap. And unlike the 1995 recession, this one proved impossible to shake off: the economy didn't grow again until 2002, when it was on the other side of a catastrophic devaluation and the biggest sovereign debt default on record. The conclusion that was reached during the course of 2001 was that the peso was irredeemably expensive, incompatible with either economic recovery or with reducing Argentina's external imbalance.

These two vulnerabilities—a large or persistent current account deficit and an overvaluation of the exchange rate—feature visibly in almost any account of the crises of the 1980s and 1990s. But it is a slippery business trying to isolate these two factors, along with pegged exchange rates, as the definitive causes of crisis during these decades.

To understand this, let's go back to Asia. Strengthening of inflation-adjusted exchange rates was almost completely absent in the buildup to Asia's crisis in 1997: the only country whose currency strengthened in a way that could be described as worrisome was the Philippines, whose real effective exchange rate appreciated by 30 percent between 1990 and 1996. In Thailand, for example, at the epicenter of Asia's crisis in 1997, the real exchange rate had appreciated by only 7 percent during the early 1990s. Then again, Thailand's current account deficit remained stubbornly high in the years running up to the crisis, reaching 8 percent of GDP during 1995 and 1996. But not so Korea, whose current account deficits were considerably smaller. Whenever one tries to generalize, up pops a counterexample.

One reason why it is so difficult to articulate a neat theory of crisis is because one of the engines of the crises during this period was contagion, or the way in which financial disturbance spreads from one country to another. We've seen the domino-like character of the crises in the 1980s and 1990s and how the March 1997 currency devaluation in the Czech Republic helped alert investors to similar risks that had built up in Thailand, whose crisis triggered others in the region, as well Russia's the following summer. And that Russian crisis set the stage for Brazil's 1999 devaluation, which helped undermine Argentina, insofar as Brazil was the market for a third of Argentina's exports.

Explaining this contagion has something to do with economic similarities: when a country with vulnerability x has a crisis, then other countries with similar vulnerabilities can become victims of capital outflows. It also has something to do with economic linkages, in the way, for example, that Argentina was a victim of Brazil's devaluation. But it also has to do with the way creditors behave. Creditors who suffer large losses from a devaluation in country x will tend to lose risk appetite and start reducing their exposure to other countries to avoid similar losses. Exactly what they choose to sell will be driven partly by existing economic similarities and linkages, but not entirely. What they choose to sell will also depend on what they own. If a portfolio manager has a very large position in the debt securities of country x at a time when countries y and z are tipping toward crisis, then she might be inclined to reduce her exposure to country x even if its vulnerabilities don't seem especially threatening.

It's the Balance Sheet, Stupid!

If one generalization is worth making about the era of emerging markets crises—or one single lesson to be learned from these episodes—it is that vulnerability is primarily contained in weak balance sheets.

The definition of balance sheet that is overwhelmingly important here is what might be called a country's external balance sheet. At the risk of oversimplifying, the asset side of that balance sheet is essentially made up of foreign exchange reserves, or the ready-to-use assets of a country's central bank, mostly denominated in U.S. dollars. (In 1995, just over 60 percent of the world's reserves were dollar-denominated; by 2015, that share had risen to just below 70 percent.) On the liabilities side is the stock of a country's foreign debt, and in particular the stock of short-term foreign debt, due within a year. In crisis after crisis during the 1990s, this balance sheet became stretched, in the sense that the stock of short-term foreign debt grew to a level considerably above the stock of foreign exchange reserves that might be needed to repay that debt if foreign creditors demanded repayment. Even syndicated bank credits of the 1970s had some of the characteristics of short-term debt because of the way in which the interest rate on these loans was repriced every three months through changes in LIBOR.

In the buildup to crises in Mexico, Thailand, Korea, the Philippines, Indonesia, Russia, Turkey, Brazil, and plenty of other countries, a pattern is visible. First, a more or less pegged exchange rate allowed policymakers and foreign investors to delude themselves into thinking that the stability of the currency could be taken for granted. Second, the relatively high interest rates that were available in the local currency encouraged local borrowers to take on dollar-denominated debt, sell those dollars, and buy a local currency–denominated obligation with a much higher yield. Or they encouraged foreign investors to sell dollars in exchange for local currency and use the proceeds to buy a local debt instrument. That "carry trade" can seem like a good idea at the time not only because of the pegged exchange rate but because of the assumption that this time is different: a country's capital account has been opened, domestic interest rates are being liberalized according to the Washington Consensus, the mood is good, and the herd is moving. An individual member of the herd thinks that he or she is smart enough to spot difficulties in a country before anyone else, and to take repayment before the central bank's reserves get exhausted. But the paradox of the herd is that this cannot be true for everyone.

And so the stock of short-term external debt grows to exceed the stock of foreign exchange reserves. Since the pegged exchange rate requires the central bank to sell dollars at the pegged rate, the trigger that causes capital flows to go into reverse drains the central bank of its reserves, with the inevitable consequence that the exchange rate devalues.

But in addition to the external balance sheet, two other balance sheets play interconnecting roles in the buildup to crisis. One is the balance sheet of the financial sector and the other is the balance sheet of the government.

Any story about large capital inflows to a country with a weak banking system will almost always end unhappily. In the mid-1990s, the most explosive combination of large-scale external financing and weak banks was found in Asia, where financial vulnerability was created as a result of low levels of capital, weak supervision, inadequate provisioning standards, and very little transparency about what banks were actually doing. A lot of domestic Asian bank lending in the 1990s was backed up by collateral. So, while property prices kept going up, a virtuous circle seemed to appear: real estate booms in Jakarta, Kuala Lumpur, Bangkok, and Manila helped build confidence about the quality of the banks' loans, and that in turn produced a bullish mentality throughout the East Asian financial sector.[26] Once a "trigger" materializes, though, expectations of falling growth hurt property values, and that in turn weakens the quality of the banks' loans, raises fears of a banking crisis, and fuels capital outflows. This in turn makes it difficult, if not impossible, for a central bank to raise interest rates decisively in an effort to protect the currency: the vulnerability of the banking system means that monetary tightening would by itself trigger a domestic crisis.

And once the devaluation takes place, those banking sector fears become a reality as bankruptcies surge among companies and banks with debts to repay in dollars that have just become hugely expensive to buy. In the 1980s and 1990s, something like half of all crises in the balance of payments were associated with a banking sector crisis.[27]

The vulnerability in the financial sector then produces vulnerability in the public sector because of the vast cost to the government of supporting the banks. The public funds required to pay for banking sector crises in developing countries have been equivalent to 10 percent of GDP on average since 1970, but the fiscal costs of the crises of the 1990s reached viscerally painful levels. Following the 1997 crises, the cost of bailing out the banking sector was equivalent to 57 percent of GDP in Indonesia, 44 percent of GDP in Thailand, and 33 percent of GDP in Korea. Bailing out Turkey's banks after its 2001 crisis cost 32 percent of GDP.[28] The costs of all this to a nation's income growth are depressing indeed: one study suggests that from the mid-1970s to 1997, a typical currency crisis would cause a country's output to fall by up to 5–8 percent and a typical banking crisis would cause a fall of up to 10–13 percent.[29]

In looking across the whole of these decades, it seems striking that lessons that might have been apparent enough after 1982 were so thoroughly unlearned by the time capital flows reappeared in the early 1990s. Those lessons were about the wisdom of avoiding pegged exchange rates, about the danger of thinking that this time is different, about the risks posed by swings in U.S. monetary conditions, about the need to share currency risk and maturity risk between borrowers and lenders, about the fickleness of banks as international lenders, and about the dangers of a rapid surge in capital inflows, on the intuitive grounds that what enters can just as easily exit.

By the early 2000s, though, it seemed that one lesson, at least, *was* learned. But this was not that the volatility of global capital flows was a problem in itself. The lesson, rather, was that developing countries were not well enough equipped to see their way through the volatility of international capital flows. In other words, it wasn't that the international financial system per se needed to be made safer for developing countries; it was that developing countries needed to do more to ensure their own safety within the international financial system. And the way in which they did that, as we shall see in the following chapter, was to make strenuous efforts to strengthen their balance sheets; balance sheet weakness, after all, had been an overwhelming source of these countries' vulnerability during the 1980s and 1990s. What started off as "this time is different" ended up as "never again."

The efforts that countries would make to strengthen their balance sheets took place despite—or perhaps because of—the role played by the IMF in helping to manage these crises. Although the IMF is often thought of as a creditors' enforcer, a more debtor-friendly approach by the IMF appeared as early as 1987, when the fund announced that it was prepared to lend money to Brazil even though the country was failing to pay interest on some of its debt to international creditors. This "lending into arrears" introduced a balance between the interests of debtor countries and those of their private creditors that would become increasingly visible in the late 1990s, partly because by that time the IMF and a country's commercial creditors were, in a sense, competing with each other for the limited resources that a country had to service its external debt. But however debtor-friendly the IMF would become—in forcing losses on creditors in Korea in late 1997 and in Brazil in 1999, and in supporting sovereign debt restructurings in Ecuador, Ukraine, and Pakistan in 1999–2000—its resources remained too small at a time of explosive growth in global capital markets.

Joseph Stiglitz, who was chair of President Bill Clinton's Council of Economic Advisers in the mid-1990s, may have been stretching the point by claiming, about Asia, that "capital account liberalization was the single most important factor leading to the crisis."[30] But the fact that these crises took place in an era of financial globalization—the first since the 1930s—can't seriously be disconnected from any account of how the crises materialized. And the opening up of developing countries to international finance was, it is safe to say, encouraged by the U.S. government from the 1970s on: Stiglitz himself tells a story of how the Clinton administration made Korean financial liberalization a condition of concluding a U.S.-Korea trade agreement.[31] At the very least, it is clear enough that the crises of the 1980s and 1990s took place within a global financial framework that was "U.S. shaped"—shaped both by the United States and, in many respects, for the United States. The consequences of this will be addressed in chapters to come.

In the end, though, we are left with a puzzle: how was it that the crises of the 1990s were so much shorter-lived than those of the 1980s? Although developing countries often went through what the Korean president Kim Young-sam described in 1997 as the "bone-carving pain" of postcrisis recession, more often than not that pain was rewarded with rapid economic recoveries. There was little sense, in the 1990s, of a "lost decade." The *Financial Times*'s economics commentator Martin Wolf was quite right, in mid-July 1997, to suggest that Thailand's crisis was "no more than a blip."[32]

This era of crises, in other words, as persistent and costly as it was, never really threatened the viability of so-called emerging markets as an asset class or as an investment theme in global capital markets. So how could a group of countries that had succumbed so consistently to financial crises be considered a proper destination for the world's money? Trying to resolve that puzzle is the task we turn to now.

THREE

Explaining Emerging Markets

WASHINGTON, 1989

Though it ended up as an infamous encapsulation of modern economic orthodoxy in developing countries, the Washington Consensus had a humble start: the two words are quietly tucked away, without capitals or quotation marks, in the second paragraph of chapter 2 of a book titled *Latin American Adjustment: How Much Has Happened?*[1] The book, edited by John Williamson, was published in 1990 but was based on a conference that had taken place the previous year. As its title suggests, the policies ascribed to the Washington Consensus were already being implemented during the 1980s, most visibly in such countries as Mexico, Chile, and Turkey. These policies were being implemented in the context of IMF programs in some cases, but mostly not. There was no "big bang," in other words, no single moment when these policies were somehow deposited, in the form of a how-to manual, on the desks of finance ministers and central bank governors. Although the consensus certainly took on the role of a set of recommendations about how developing countries should steer their economic policy, it started life mostly as a description of policies that had been gradually acquiring wider acceptance.

The revolution in economic policymaking that is captured by the words "Washington Consensus"—summarized by Williamson as "prudent macroeconomic policies, outward orientation, and free-market capitalism"[2]—goes a long way toward helping resolve the puzzle that ended the previous chapter of this book. The scars left by repeated financial crises didn't turn capital permanently away from developing countries. On the contrary: capital kept coming back. And the reason it did so is explained by the fact that these crises did nothing to turn developing countries away from participating in the global economy.

The problems that countries faced during the era of crises had little to do with the case for *economic* globalization, or how a country takes part in a global market for goods and services. Rather, they had everything to do with how to manage *financial* globalization, which describes how a country takes part in a global market for money and capital. Economic globalization is of course inseparable from financial globalization to some degree; trying to have one entirely without the other is a bit like trying to swim in an empty pool. But though developing countries manifestly need some kind of interaction with global finance in order to participate meaningfully in the global economy, the question remains as to how the interaction should be managed. The aim of this chapter is to describe how that question was answered in the wake of two decades of financial crises.

It is on the subject of financial globalization that, moreover, the Washington Consensus needs a bit of careful understanding. What we will see in this chapter is a distinction between Williamson's own Washington Consensus, which was rather suspicious of financial globalization *except* for the flow of FDI, and the Washington Consensus as it was understood by the likes of the IMF and the U.S. Treasury, institutions that displayed enthusiasm for the unfettered mobility of global capital in more or less all its forms. Washington's view, not Williamson's, prevailed. That simple fact had a huge effect on the behavior of developing countries: they sought to protect themselves from the volatility of global capital flows. And the result of that effort is that the concept of emerging markets—shorthand for the interaction between developing countries and global capital—remained coherent as a theme for global investors, and kept on growing in prominence.

Globalizations Past and Present

Though it would be wrong to argue that the policies summarized in the Washington Consensus were imposed on developing countries in a kind of conspiracy, it is fair to say that the word "Washington" here reasonably implies some sort of official encouragement of these policies: from the U.S. Treasury, the U.S. Federal Reserve, the IMF, the World Bank, the Inter-American Development Bank, and the host of government agencies, think tanks, and consulting firms that populate the U.S. capital.

Nor was this the first time that American thinking had shaped economic policies abroad. In an earlier part of the "American century," Washington had been influential in shaping the economic policies of developing countries during an era of economic and financial globalization. Edwin Walter Kemmerer was a professor at Princeton University who became famous in the 1920s as an "international money doctor," doling out economic advice on "Kemmerer Missions" to Colombia, Chile, Poland, Ecuador, China, Peru, and a host of other countries.[3] It was Kemmerer, for example, who set the framework for establishing Colombia's central bank, Banco de la República, in 1923. And it was Kemmerer whose advice delivered financial stabilization to Poland during the 1920s. Since the United States had emerged from World War I as the dominant supplier of external funding for developing countries, the Kemmerer Missions nudged countries toward the best way to maximize their share of that funding; and to use the proceeds responsibly.

The advice that Kemmerer dispensed to developing countries in the 1920s was built on two main principles. The first was about the need for "sound money": responsible government finances, balanced budgets, the freeing of central banks from political control. And the second was about the relationship between international trade and foreign investment. In an article titled "The Theory of Foreign Investments," Kemmerer concluded: "Trade follows . . . investment, and the flow of investment capital together with the return flow of investment profits are substantial items in the foreign trade of an economically new country."[4]

"Sound money" and the link between trade and direct investment have strong echoes in the modern Washington Consensus. Indeed, the Kemmerer Missions themselves have an almost direct parallel with missions undertaken in the late 1980s and early 1990s by the then Harvard professor Jeffrey Sachs, whose success in advising the Bolivian government about how to curb inflation—which had reached 23,000 percent in September 1985— led to advisory mandates in Poland, Slovenia, and Russia. Sachs's advice, like that of Kemmerer, focused firmly on a regime of fiscal and monetary discipline combined with an end to economic regulation that protected elites and blocked the free market. The "shock therapy" for which Sachs became famous was based on the idea that reform in developing countries was better achieved through a quick adoption of economic ideas brought in from abroad, rather than a slow promotion of domestic alternatives. By 1993, the *New York Times* could get away with describing him as "probably the most important economist in the world."[5]

Neither Kemmerer nor Sachs worked for the U.S. government. But the ideas that each of them helped to spread were ones that were dominant in U.S. thinking about policy during their respective eras. Each of them was, in his own way, a funnel through which ideas about sound money and trade were distributed to policymakers in developing countries. And at one level, the Washington Consensus is simply a distillation of the ideas that were filtered to developing countries in the 1980s and 1990s.

The need for new ideas about policymaking in developing countries was painfully obvious in the 1980s. At the point at which these countries lurched toward debt crisis in the early part of that decade, their mode of thinking about economic policy was in some ways still the product of the 1930s: state-centered, inward-looking, and generally ill prepared for a newly globalizing world.

The 1930s had left developing countries in default on their external debt, cut off from international capital markets, lacking foreign exchange, and facing catastrophic declines in commodity prices. This experience had an effect on their thinking about economic policy that lasted for decades. In the first place, it made countries very unhappy about depending on primary commodities as the basis for income growth. This unhappiness was enshrined as "commodity pessimism," or the idea that the terms of trade for commodity-exporting countries were destined to keep falling. That view was molded during the late 1940s into the Prebisch-Singer hypothesis, which claimed that the world's demand for primary goods would inevitably expand less rapidly than its demand for industrial goods, leaving commodity exporters doomed to become relatively poor, not least because synthetic substitutes for primary commodities—rayon for cotton, aluminum for wood, polymers for natural rubber—were becoming increasingly available to consumers.[6]

Another legacy of the 1930s was an overall nervousness about financial markets—partly explained by the collapse of international capital flows at the end of the 1920s—and a growing faith in the power of the state, thanks to what seemed like success on the part of central planners in the Soviet Union.[7] Faced with a choice between the apparent fruits of investment-heavy Soviet planning, on the one hand, and the reality of capitalist chaos on the other, the intellectual tide moved away from the outward-looking orientation of Kemmerer and toward something that aspired more to national self-reliance.

If you add "commodity pessimism" to the economic nationalism that had started to become fashionable in the 1930s, what you end up with is the economic strategy adopted by numerous countries, from Brazil to Iran, in the 1950s and 1960s: import-substituting industrialization, or just ISI. Fearing that free-trade policies would lock them into an immiserizing dependence on commodities, developing country policymakers decided to escape the prospect of a rotten deal in unstable world markets, preferring instead to make a bid for national autonomy by ending the import of industrial goods and seeking to build home-grown industrial capacity.

An additional supposed advantage of an import-substituting approach to growth was that it seemed at home in a postwar world in which cross-border flows of private capital were constrained under the international monetary regime that had been born at Bretton Woods in 1944. Controls on capital movements under the Bretton Woods regime were essential to its functioning, and so the movement of private capital across borders was pretty insignificant. And if external financing isn't readily available, an import-substituting economic strategy makes some sense: striving to rely less on imports isn't a bad idea when it is difficult to locate financing for them.

To support this dream of "industrialisation in one country," an entire network was constructed in the 1950s and 1960s of tariffs, import licenses, preferential exchange rates for raw materials, cheap government loans, energy subsidies, public equity injections, and price ceilings on food to keep wages low for urban employers. The strategy, frankly, delivered some awful results. By the late 1960s, for example, the annual output of cars and trucks in eight Latin American countries was produced by a total of *ninety* firms, each with an average output of 6,700 vehicles![8] Even Raúl Prebisch, the godfather of inward-looking industrialization, had recanted by the mid-1960s and started to argue in favor of export promotion and outward orientation for developing countries.[9]

State-centered ISI looked like a failure by the early 1970s, and indeed, this was the decade in which developing countries first started to deepen their trade connections with the rest of the world: economic globalization became attractive again. At the start of the 1970s, the sum of exports plus imports in developing countries was equal to around one-fifth of their GDP. By the end of the decade, that had increased to one-third. Even in Latin America, which was relatively slow to discover trade, the ratio of total trade to GDP rose from 20 percent to around 25 percent by the end of the 1970s.

So the globalization of developing countries through trade coincided with their globalization through finance: the 1970s saw, as we learned in chapter 1, the first encounter between international capital and developing countries since the 1930s. But as we also saw, the petrodollars that helped give birth to the modern era of globalization also helped reinvigorate the role of the state during that decade. Import substitution died a quicker death, in other words, than the state's role in the economy. A more open, outward-looking strategy that put the private sector at the center of the economy was something that the 1980s debt crisis forced onto much of the developing world. That was because the net capital outflows that these countries suffered had the effect of both making the "big state" unaffordable and rendering their currencies cheaper, which in turn helped make an export-led development strategy worth more serious consideration.

But it wasn't just the disciplining effects of the 1980s debt crisis that forced a change in developing countries' economic policies. An intellectual revolution had taken place in the United Kingdom and the United States under Prime Minister Margaret Thatcher and President Ronald Reagan, itself partly influenced by the decisive shift toward free markets and the outward-looking policies under the Chilean government of Pinochet. And there was also a remarkable demonstration effect coming from countries such as Korea and Taiwan, which had begun adopting export-oriented growth strategies in the 1960s and seemed to be doing just fine: Korea's average GDP growth rate during the 1970s was 10.5 percent, around double the average growth rate for developing countries as a whole. To see how central a role exports played in Korea's growth strategy, we need only consider that the value of exports had been equal to just 7 percent of Korean GDP in 1965 but by 1981 had grown to equal 30 percent of GDP. For comparison, Brazil's ratio of exports to GDP in 1965 was the same as Korea's, 7 percent, but by 1981 it had risen to no more than 9 percent.

For all these reasons, the idea of putting trade at the center of thinking about economic policy gathered pace in the 1980s. The tariff walls built to support import substitution came tumbling down. In the early 1980s, developing countries had an average import tariff of 33 percent (and as much as 65 percent in India). But by the mid-1990s, that average tariff had fallen to 19 percent, and it fell further, to 13 percent, by 2000.[10] Nor was it just tariffs that were disappearing but an entire web of protection. As late as 1982, for example, any import into Mexico required a license. By 1990, only 14 percent of imports were burdened in that way.[11]

This reorientation of economic policy toward exports is precisely what the Washington Consensus was trying to encourage. In some ways, outward-looking economics is the heart of the Washington Consensus. Much else of what is in it—budget discipline, the freeing up of interest rates, privatization, deregulation, and the security of property rights—is just a set of policies that are complementary to the central goal of participating in a global economy instead of staying stuck inside a national one.

But promoting trade isn't sufficient. Economic globalization can't live in a vacuum; financial globalization is its unavoidable partner. In this way the role of FDI flows into developing countries became inextricably connected to trade. Writing in 1992, the economist Rüdiger Dornbusch nicely illustrated the link between opening up to trade and opening up to FDI: "Multinationals can bring direct foreign investment, but under cover of tariffs and quotas they may not do their best. Thus, today in Argentina, the 1964 Ford Falcon is still being produced with the US machinery of that time, without model change, as if the clock had stopped."[12]

In other words, the liberalization of trade and the inflow of FDI feed off each other. This was pretty clearly grasped by Professor Kemmerer in the 1920s, but it became spectacularly true in the modern era of globalization. It is not merely that outward-looking economics benefits from the technology transfer that can become available through FDI but also that the rise in imports that follows tariff cuts needs to be financed; inflows of FDI can help finance that increase in the import bill.

The rise of trade and the rise in FDI flows, then, were the twins of modern globalization for developing countries. On the one hand, the growth in trade supported growth in FDI flows. Falling tariffs proved in the 1990s to be a powerful magnet for inflows of FDI, particularly where those tariff reductions took place in the context of free-trade agreements.[13] And on the other hand, FDI flows supported an increase in trade. In Malaysia, for example, while 26 percent of exports were sold by foreign-owned firms in 1985, that share had risen to 45 percent ten years later. By 1999, 80 percent of Hungary's exports were sold by foreign-owned firms.[14]

FDI is the bedrock of financial globalization; it goes together with an outward-looking economic strategy. Other types of capital flow—international bank lending, portfolio investments in local bond markets or stock markets—are in some sense superficial to this. So, during the current era of globalization, it is probably to be welcomed that FDI has been the dominant form of capital flowing into developing countries. Between 1990 and 2015, the total net inflow of private sector capital into these countries averaged around 4.4 percent of GDP per year, and net inflows of FDI have accounted for almost half that, or 2.1 percent of GDP. In dollar terms, total net private capital flows during these years amounted to nearly $14 trillion. Net flows of FDI were a little under $7 trillion.

On "Good" and "Bad" Kinds of Capital Flows

Here we encounter a problem. Few economists disagree with the proposition that an outward-looking economic strategy is generally better for developing countries than the inward-looking variety that gave rise to ISI. Not too many people seriously entertain the idea that we should return to a world in which Latin America has ninety car companies that are doomed, through protectionism, to fail to achieve any kind of economies of scale. Equally, few economists disagree with the idea that trade flows naturally go hand in hand with flows of FDI. But the problem is this: despite the dominant role played by FDI in the structure of capital flows to developing countries during the past thirty years, there is precious little evidence that links financial globalization to income gains in these countries. Or, to quote the most comprehensive study of the academic analysis of this question, "The vast empirical literature provides little robust evidence of a causal relationship between financial integration and growth."[15] A related conclusion about capital flows and growth looks at the volatility of consumption spending in developing countries. In principle, access to financing is supposed to reduce the volatility of consumer spending since the whole point of borrowing is that it allows spending to be smoothed over time. But it seems that for developing countries, the opposite may have happened: the volatility of consumption growth actually increased.[16] The costs of financial globalisation seem all too clear—two decades of financial crisis provide plenty of scope to argue that capital flows can be bad for you—but the benefits are trickier to pin down.

One way of navigating through this debate is to latch on to the idea that there is a hierarchy of capital flows: some are better than others. And one way of defining that hierarchy is to consider the volatility of these flows, or the ease and frequency with which money comes and goes. Within that hierarchy, flows of FDI are usually judged to be a winner when compared with debt-creating flows. A simple illustration of this is what happened in Asia after the 1997 crisis. During the four years that followed, Asian countries (excluding China) said goodbye to $80 billion as foreign banks continued to take repayments on largely short-term cross-border lending that had been extended to these countries during the boom. But during the same period, there was a net inflow of FDI to the tune of $90 billion.[17]

An important feature of FDI is that the payments that flow out of a country from a direct investment have "risk-sharing" characteristics. If you owe a dollar of debt to a foreign creditor, you owe that dollar no matter whether your economy is capable of actually producing a dollar, either by earning it through exports or by borrowing it from someone else. But the dividend payments that flow from a direct investment will flow only if the economy is growing. In a sense, then, FDI sits at the opposite end of the spectrum from short-term external debt.

And FDI has some other attractive characteristics. It is the one form of capital flow that promises economic benefits that, in theory at least, should be measurable: by transferring technology, it offers the chance to improve the productivity of a country's existing stock of capital. This is a view powerfully promoted by the Chinese, whose use of FDI features in the next chapter.

All that said, it would be wrong to view FDI as an entirely risk-free form of financing. And the story of FDI flows into the financial sector of developing countries helps make this point.

From the late 1990s, the flow of FDI into the banking systems of developing countries was dramatic: the share of banks' balance sheets in these countries that ultimately was held by foreign banks grew from 22 percent in 1996 to 39 percent by 2005.[18] The case for the defense of this kind of FDI is that healthy foreign banks can bring in capital and technical skills to a developing country's financial sector, promote competition, and help lower the risk of boom-and-bust financial cycles. One reason for this might be that if there is a sudden loss of confidence in the local currency, foreign-owned banks might be the destination for local capital flight, instead of this capital leaving the country. There is sometimes an argument to be made that foreign banks cherry-pick among local borrowers, choosing to lend to only the best and leaving local banks having to lend to less creditworthy firms and households. But the tone of most of the academic analysis of this subject is that financial sector FDI is, by and large, okay.

Nowhere did financial sector FDI become more visible than in Central and Eastern Europe, and yet equally, maybe no other region has suffered more from its unpleasant side effects. By the time of the global financial crisis in 2008, the banking sectors of the Baltic states were almost entirely foreign-owned, Bulgaria's banks were 85 percent foreign-owned, and Hungary's were 75 percent foreign-owned. But this region also contains some of the countries that suffered most from the effects of the crisis: Romania's real GDP contracted by 7 percent in 2009; Ukraine's GDP contracted by almost 15 percent. Both countries, along with Hungary and Bulgaria, had to turn to the IMF to find a new source of funding.

Did financial sector FDI play a role in destabilizing Central and Eastern Europe in the run-up to the 2008 crisis? To an extent, yes, because of the ease with which foreign-owned banks in the region could finance themselves by borrowing offshore. By early 2008, these countries had accumulated almost $1 trillion in cross-border liabilities owed to international banks, up from just $250 billion in 2003. Much of this debt arose from parent banks in the United States and Western Europe making loans to their subsidiaries in

Central and Eastern Europe. A sharp buildup of external debt like this arguably should have triggered a warning, particularly since a good deal of the borrowing was channeled toward providing foreign currency mortgages to Central European households. By 2007, over half the debt of households in Hungary and Romania, for example, was denominated in foreign currencies. Here was another example of the "this time is different" phenomenon: the prospect of income convergence with Western Europe, and the expectation of strengthening local currencies, lured both creditors and debtors into thinking that large increases in foreign currency debt were tolerable. And as many of these countries were new members of the EU, and thereby committed to one day joining the eurozone, they may have anticipated that the risk involved in borrowing foreign currencies might vanish if the debts would eventually be repaid in euros. What all this suggests is that the dark side of FDI is largely the result of the way it opened a door to excessive foreign borrowing, a problem with which developing countries had become all too familiar during the 1970s and 1990s.

An additional problem, arguably, is that FDI flows to the developing world have been spread across a relatively narrow range of countries. Since 1990, a fifth of the entire flow of FDI to developing countries went to China alone, and four-fifths of the whole flow was captured by a total of just twenty-five countries. Brazil, Mexico, Russia, India, and Chile by themselves accounted for a quarter of the entire FDI flow to developing countries during this period.

On balance, though, it is worth emphasizing that FDI is, broadly speaking, a "friendly" form of capital inflow: it adds to the production of goods and services, it doesn't exit a country quickly, and its returns tend to be paid to investors only when the economy is growing. But the very idea that FDI is friendly carries us a long way from the 1970s, when foreign bank loans seemed preferable to inflows of FDI on the ground that they constituted less of an assault on a country's sovereignty. During the 1990s and 2000s, by contrast, a more common belief was that some sacrifice of sovereignty—in the form of allowing parts of one's economy to be owned by foreigners—might not be a bad trade-off for the benefits of globalization.

In the end, though, the modern history of capital flows to developing countries can be described as the triumph of FDI over other forms of capital. FDI has replaced debt as the most significant liability on the external balance sheet of developing countries. One reason why this helped to keep emerging markets intact as an asset class, despite the apparent endlessness of crises in the 1980s and 1990s, is that inflows of FDI are more likely to produce what one set of economists has called "collateral benefits."[19] The idea is that while the ability of foreign direct investors to pack their bags and move elsewhere may not have visible effects on growth, it may encourage governments to introduce policies that support development in the long run. Foreign investors may be more likely to stick around in a country where contracts are enforceable, where the financial system isn't plagued by corruption or low levels of capital, where corruption in general is kept at levels that are short of endemic, and where policymaking is conducted transparently. If these are the positive side effects of a country opening itself up to foreign capital, then financial globalization may be worthwhile even if its contribution to economic growth is difficult to identify.

On "Good" and "Bad" Kinds of Washington Consensus

Though John Williamson coined the term Washington Consensus in 1989, the concept acquired a life of its own that didn't quite meet its originator's expectations. As Williamson had conceived it, the only form of external financing that was explicitly encouraged in the Washington Consensus was FDI. As he put it in 1990, "A restrictive attitude limiting the entry of foreign direct investment (FDI) is . . . foolish," in view of the benefits it might confer in the form of technology transfer and financing with risk-sharing characteristics. In other words, Williamson's Washington Consensus "did not, quite deliberately, extend to liberalisation of *all* capital inflows, or, for that matter, capital outflows" (emphasis added).[20]

However, that's not quite how things evolved. Williamson's view of the Washington Consensus was not Washington's view of the Washington Consensus. In fact, it is probably worth making a distinction between what might be deemed the "pure" Washington Consensus, the one defined by Williamson himself, and an "impure" one, the form that seeped into the general consciousness of policymakers, market participants, and economists. In a general sense, the impure Washington Consensus was the one that became synonymous with neoliberalism or market fundamentalism. This was not what Williamson had in mind, and indeed, he described this view as a "thoroughly objectionable perversion" of his original meaning.[21] In a more specific sense, the impure consensus gave priority to the full liberalization of the capital accounts of developing countries—also not what Williamson had had in mind.

The reason why these two versions of the Washington Consensus could exist side by side lies in the fact that the consensus itself slips between what could be called descriptive and prescriptive modes. A hint of this gap was already on display at the 1989 conference at which Williamson's paper was delivered. Stanley Fischer, at the time the chief economist of the World Bank, responded to Williamson's paper by commenting, "I fear rather that much of Washington does believe strongly that financial capital flows should not be constrained."[22]

Indeed, that was the case. As far as the U.S. Treasury was concerned, full global capital mobility was a more or less unalloyed good. As U.S. treasury secretary in 2000, Larry Summers compared international capital mobility with international travel by aircraft. As he put it:

> The jet airplane made air travel more comfortable, more efficient, and more safe, though the accidents were more spectacular and for a time more numerous after the jet was invented. In the same way, modern global financial markets carry with them enormous potential for benefit, even if some of the accidents are that much more spectacular. As the right public policy response to the jet was longer runways, better air-traffic control, and better training for pilots, and the discouragement of rapid travel, so the right public policy response to financial innovation is to assure a safe framework so that the benefits can be realized, not to stifle the change.[23]

The U.S. preference for open capital accounts wasn't simply expressed as a view that could be taken or left; it extended to actual policymaking. Joseph Stiglitz, for example, who ended up believing that capital account liberalization was the single most important factor in creating the Asian crisis, recalled that when he was working in Bill Clinton's White House, the government of Korea came under pressure from Washington to accelerate financial and capital market liberalization in exchange for a U.S.-Korea trade deal.[24] Ditto with Chile: the U.S.-Chile Free Trade Agreement reached in 2003 put limits on Chile's ability to impose capital controls in the future.[25]

Perhaps the most enthusiastic and explicit supporter of capital account liberalization was the IMF. On the face of it, this seems odd. The IMF was born in a world in which the idea of controlling international capital movements was at the very heart of the international monetary system set up at the 1944 Bretton Woods conference, and was influenced by the memory of the crises wrought by unfettered global capital mobility in the 1920s. Indeed, Article VI, Section 3 of the IMF's Articles of Agreement specifies that member states "may exercise such controls as are necessary to regulate international capital movements."

During the early 1990s, however, what the IMF preached had increasingly little to do with this assertion. As the IMF itself acknowledged later on, it "viewed capital account liberalization favorably in its country work" from the beginning of the decade.[26] It is as if the IMF, witnessing the rise in capital flows to developing countries that occurred in the early 1990s, was either unable or unwilling to look back to the 1980s debt crises in order to learn anything about the risks that volatile capital flows might generate for the developing countries on the receiving end of them.

The IMF's role as cheerleader for a world of wholly mobile international capital reached a climax in 1997. In the early part of that year, as the Thai stock market was falling and as the Czech crisis in March was alerting the world to the risks of short-term capital, appreciated currencies, and large current account deficits, the IMF was giving shape to a proposed amendment to its Articles of Agreement that would have given the fund a new purpose: formally to promote the liberalization of international capital flows. Article VI, Section 3 would have been rewritten thus: "Members shall not, without the approval of the Fund, impose restrictions on the making of payments and transfers for international capital transactions."[27]

The timing of this proposal was unfortunate in view of what was building in Asia. Yet even after the Asian crisis exploded in the summer of 1997, officials gathered at the annual meeting of the IMF and World Bank in September of that year to consider the proposed amendment. In a speech he gave to justify the proposal, Fischer, by then the IMF's first deputy managing director, offered the argument that countries would be allowed to impose controls on capital flows during a transition period, but only under the umbrella of a "code of good behavior in the application of capital controls."[28] The IMF's stubbornness on the issue of capital account openness remained on show in early 1998, when Michel Camdessus, the IMF's managing director, spoke once again in defense of giving the IMF jurisdiction over capital movements.[29]

As the Asian crisis morphed into the Russian crisis, however, and the Russian crisis morphed into the Brazil crisis, the proposed amendment died a quiet death. But even though the IMF stepped back from the idea of amending its articles to give it a role in guiding the world toward fully mobile capital movements, Washington as a whole seemed to remain wedded to the notion that restricting capital movements should be avoided. Or to put it another way: Washington, unlike Williamson, just didn't much like capital controls.

Capital, Interrupted

Any discussion of capital controls should be careful to distinguish between controlling capital *inflows*, on the one hand, and controlling *outflows* on the other. If a country has put in place controls on capital inflows, then an investor broadly knows in advance on what terms he or she will be committing funds. On the other hand, the imposition of controls on capital outflows can introduce a contractual or financial uncertainty, as investors may suddenly find themselves unable to get their money out of the country.

The canonical example of controls on capital inflows is the regime that Chile had in place between 1991 and 1998. Chile was faced with the same early 1990s surge in capital inflows that set the stage for the Mexican crisis a few years later. In contrast to many other countries, though, Chile tried to impose some kind of barrier. From June 1991, any foreign lender to Chile was required to deposit 20 percent of the loan in question into an account at the Central Bank that received no interest. This stipulation was called an unremunerated reserve requirement, or URR. Moreover, foreign investors had to wait three years to take their capital out. The terms were changed slightly the following summer, when the URR was raised to 30 percent and the minimum stay was cut to two years.[30] By 1998, when volatile capital was rushing from emerging markets as a result of the Asian crisis, Chile's capital controls were simply allowed to lapse.

There is heated debate as to whether or not Chile's controls were successful. Certainly there were arguments that taxing capital inflows through the reserve requirement made the domestic cost of borrowing higher than it might otherwise have been, as a larger inflow might have put more downward pressure on local interest rates. But if the goal of the controls was to insulate Chile from the dangers of running up large stocks of short-term external debt, the experiment must be considered a success. In 1990 the stock of Chile's short-term external debt amounted to just under 20 percent of its total external debt. By 1996 the share had fallen to just 12 percent.[31] Chile was nowhere near the center of turmoil when the Asian crisis struck the following year. Controlling capital inflows may not work forever, since investors will search hard for loopholes through which to avoid such restrictions. But seven years of success in Chile's case is not a bad track record.

In contrast to Chile's approach to controlling capital inflows is the approach that Malaysia took to controlling capital outflows in September 1998, when it introduced a raft of restrictions to protect its currency and try to escape the ravages of a crisis that by then had seen the exchange rate fall by 25 percent in inflation-adjusted, trade-weighted terms and real per capita GDP fall by 10 percent. The authorities forbade nonresidents from borrowing the Malaysian ringgit, to stop investors from shorting the currency; introduced a 12-month waiting period for nonresidents to convert ringgit proceeds from the sale of any Malaysian securities (bonds or stocks); and forced Malaysians to seek approval, above a certain limit, to invest abroad for any reason.

Superficially, the Malaysian controls could be described as a success. Their introduction coincided with a disappearance of pressure on the currency, and so the central bank's decision to peg the ringgit's exchange rate to the U.S. dollar at 3.8—which it did on the day it introduced the capital controls—wasn't confronted by any effort in the foreign exchange market to price the dollar at a more expensive rate. Of course, one reason why that might have been the case was that the authorities had just introduced controls on capital outflows, and so the ability to buy dollars had been squeezed by the authorities' regulatory effort.

But it is also tempting to argue that the *willingness* to buy dollars had also disappeared in Malaysia by the summer of 1998: dollars had become so expensive, thanks to the ringgit's depreciation, that no one really wanted to buy them any more, particularly since the imposition of capital controls took place at a moment when all the money seeking to exit the country had had plenty of time in which to do so. In other words, Malaysia's capital controls might have been "effective" simply because they just weren't necessary by the time they were imposed.

Whether or not Malaysia's capital controls worked in any meaningful sense, the more important feature of this story is the political background against which they were introduced. Prime Minister Mahathir Mohamad had effectively declared war against unrestricted capital mobility, in particular accusing the "great powers"—the United States, in other words— of forcing Asian countries to open their markets and then manipulating their currencies in some form of conspiracy. Mahathir's judgment was that currency trading was "unnecessary, unproductive, and totally immoral. It should be stopped. It should be made illegal. We don't need currency trading."[32] That in turn put the United States on the defensive, eliciting a response from U.S. treasury secretary Robert Rubin, who felt compelled to defend currency trading as "integral to global trade in goods and services."[33]

One legacy of the Asian crisis was, in fact, to push Washington toward a more sympathetic view of restrictions on capital mobility. Even Rubin expresses some sympathy for them in his autobiography.[34] But that change of mood took time. As things evolved in the late 1990s and early 2000s, the era of crises did little to make restrictions on capital mobility an acceptable tool to reduce the probability of crises in the future. The impure version of the Washington Consensus, with its emphasis on fully open capital accounts, remained intact. At a World Bank seminar in late 1997, Larry Summers was asked why Washington didn't favor more Chilean-type efforts to restrict capital inflows. His reply: "It's kind of like telling an alcoholic that a little bit of wine is good for your health. It may be true, but you don't want to tell him."[35]

The reasons why a country might want to impose capital controls have been nicely summarized as "four fears": a fear of currency appreciation, a fear of excessive "hot money," a fear of being overwhelmed by foreign capital, and a fear of losing autonomy over monetary policy.[36] At the end of the 1990s, it wasn't really the done thing to address any of these fears by restricting capital mobility. Then again, from the point of view of developing countries, there was little prospect that global capital flows would become any less volatile or problematic.

Wrapping Up Warmly

What was to be done? How should countries cope with these fears? The answer, in short, was self-help.[37] Since there would be no broad agreement to restrict capital flows to make international finance safe for developing countries, developing countries therefore had to ensure their own safety within international financial markets. And they equally had little reason to put much faith in the IMF's ability to deliver resources to make crises less likely. The conditions to which IMF lending was attached had become politically toxic for many countries, and a country's creditors couldn't take much confidence from the announcement that it had reached an agreement with the IMF, since an agreement by itself did not necessarily mean that funds would be disbursed according to any particular schedule. In any case, the IMF's track record in preventing crisis wasn't terribly convincing: its precrisis loans to Russia in the summer of 1998 and to Argentina in the summer of 2001 had failed to deliver those countries from collapse.

So developing countries had to wrap up warmly, had to insulate themselves from the inclement financial weather produced by the volatile movements of international capital. These efforts to protect themselves took a number of forms during the years that followed the crises of the late 1990s, but the simplest way of summarizing them is that they all amounted to balance-sheet strengthening. This is the corollary of the idea that it was, above all, balance sheet weakness that made developing countries vulnerable to crises in the 1980s and 1990s.

By far the most visible form of balance sheet strengthening was the accumulation of foreign exchange reserves. Having access to one's own source of internationally accepted liquidity seemed to be the key to financial autonomy in a world of volatile capital flows. Keeping hold of that kind of liquidity was not a completely new idea, of course. In the late 1970s it was common to think that developing countries should hold on to a stock of reserves equal to three months' spending on imports. But defining reserves adequacy in these terms no longer seemed sufficient in the 1990s. By then, international liquidity seemed more necessary to shore up the *capital* account of the balance of payments than the current account.

In 1999 Alan Greenspan, the U.S. Fed chair, popularized an idea that had been circulating among policymakers for a couple of years: "Countries should manage their external assets and liabilities in such a way that they are always able to live without new foreign borrowing for up to one year."[38] Put another way: make sure your foreign exchange reserves are at least equal to your stock of external debt that might need to be repaid within the coming year. This became known as the Greenspan-Guidotti rule, and seemed like an appropriate upgrade of the three months' import cover rule of thumb.

What actually happened to foreign exchange reserves during the twenty years that followed the Asian crisis made the Greenspan-Guidotti rule look rather puny, however. In mid-1997, developing countries—excluding China; we'll come back to that—held a total of $325 billion in foreign exchange reserves, equivalent to around 90 percent of their short-term debt. By the middle of 2017 that stock of reserves had risen to $2.5 trillion, or the equivalent of 350 percent of short-term external debt. Not only was Greenspan's rule surpassed, it was surpassed to an absurd extreme.

Why did the stock of reserves in developing countries reach such heights? The best way to think of the process is as a kind of circular, self-reinforcing one. The immediate aftermath of the 1990s crises left developing countries with cheap currencies and current account surpluses. This was the natural consequence of the capital outflows they had suffered, which devalue a country's currency and force it to avoid running current account deficits that the world is no longer willing to finance. In 1999, emerging economies as a whole had a current account surplus for the first time since 1980. But those current account surpluses didn't slip back into deficits once capital flows returned: developing countries rather liked the idea of running a current account surplus, as this helped eliminate one of the sources of vulnerability that had become so evident in the 1980s and 1990s.

And since hanging on to a current account surplus requires keeping your currency relatively cheap, central banks in developing countries found that buying dollars and building up reserves was a convenient way of achieving a number of objectives. Central bank purchases of dollars in the foreign exchange market helped stop currencies from appreciating excessively, which in turn helped sustain current account surpluses, which in turn delivered self-help, or self-insurance, in the form of reserves accumulation.

After 1999, this process seemed to develop into a kind of addiction. Developing countries, taken as a whole, ran a current account surplus every year from 1999 until 2011. Since the "normal" economics of a developing country suggest that it should be importing capital from the rest of the world—and running a current account deficit as a result of that—to fund industrial modernization, what we've seen in recent years has turned economics on its head. It has also turned history on its head: previously, developing countries had run current account deficits for almost all of the historical period for which data exist.

These current account surpluses provided a good chunk of the dollars that ended up on central banks' balance sheets in the form of foreign exchange reserves. Between 1999 and 2014, the accumulated current account surplus of developing countries (excluding China) amounted to something over $850 billion, which financed more than a quarter of the $3 trillion increase in their foreign exchange reserves. In other words, the emerging economies' postcrisis desire to wrap up warmly led them not just toward an increase in foreign exchange reserves but to an entirely different way of thinking about what it would take to protect themselves against volatile capital flows.

Reserve accumulation took on its addictive quality because judging when to stop is no simple task. One reason for this is that there is a competitive element to building up reserves: if you have more than I have, investors will judge you as more creditworthy, allowing you to borrow abroad at lower rates than I can. That might encourage me to accumulate even more reserves. Equally, if you are accumulating reserves, you might be more successful than I in preventing your currency from strengthening, and that might give you a competitive advantage. In a world in which there is no objective, or absolute, way of telling when enough reserves are enough, a country will tend to think that the right way of assessing the adequacy of its reserves is relative to other countries. Of course, not all countries have been able or even willing to participate in the reserves grab of the past twenty years. The South African Reserve Bank, for example, remained confident for a long time that its willingness to let its currency float meant that it didn't need a large stock of foreign reserves. But by the mid-2000s, South Africa had become convinced by sovereign rating agencies that their assessment of the country's creditworthiness would be stronger if South Africa had more reserves.

And in their efforts to suppress currency appreciation by intervening in domestic foreign exchange markets, developing-country central banks were holding true to one of the original tenets of Williamson's Washington Consensus: to maintain an exchange rate "sufficiently competitive to induce a rapid growth in non-traditional exports."[39] As we saw in earlier chapters, currency competitiveness was sometimes an elusive goal in the 1970s, 1980s, and 1990s as policymakers often preferred to use the exchange rate as an inflation-stabilizing tool, with the result that currencies became progressively more expensive in real terms. The era of reserves accumulation has, marginally at least, helped support developing countries' competitiveness.

Balance sheet strengthening went further than building up assets in the form of foreign exchange reserves; it also affected how governments in the developing world thought about their liabilities, or public debt. Currency depreciation and rising interest rates had pushed up the burden of government debt in many developing countries during the late 1990s and early 2000s. In 2003, the IMF issued a warning that reflected a widely held view at the time: "The increase in public debt to high levels in many emerging market economies in recent years has once again raised concerns about debt sustainability and whether there could be a repeat of the 1980s debt crisis."[40] As if in response to this warning, the ratio of public debt to GDP in developing countries declined sharply thereafter. In 2002 the average public debt/GDP ratio was around 62 percent. By 2008, it was 34 percent.

All this brings us to an important paradox. Relatively cheap currencies, current account surpluses, growing stocks of reserves, and declining stocks of public debt all helped make developing countries ever more creditworthy in the years that followed the crises of the late 1990s. And so long as international investors could expect creditworthiness to keep on improving, they became more willing to invest.

As a result, the more effort developing countries made to insulate themselves from the volatility of international capital flows, the more capital kept on coming in. This, more than any arguments about the "collateral benefits" of financial globalization, might be the real underlying force that kept the emerging markets proposition intact during the era of crises. And to be sure, countries were rewarded with increased inflows of portfolio capital, particularly into the markets for local government bonds. In 2002, for example, foreign investors owned only 2 percent of the peso-denominated bonds issued by the Mexican government. By 2016, that share of ownership had risen to 35 percent. In Indonesia, from zero holdings in 2002, foreign investors had come to own 40 percent of the government's rupiah-denominated bonds by 2016. Increasingly, some of those foreign investors are, indirectly at least, the central banks of other developing countries. A central bank will pay an asset manager to invest some of its reserves, and so its own foreign exchange reserves constitute some of the inflow into other developing countries' bond markets. By one estimate, some 5 percent of the inflow into developing countries' bond markets comes in as a result of "south-south" investment, from one developing country to another.[41]

What was the cost of all this effort to buy reserves and reduce public debt burdens? When it comes to thinking about reserves accumulation, economists emphasize a couple of different issues. One is the cost of what is known as sterilizing the purchase of reserves. Because a central bank sells its own currency to buy dollars, the creation of that local currency will increase the country's money supply—with possible inflationary consequences—unless the central bank withdraws that currency from circulation by exchanging it for something like a bond, which isn't included in the money supply. But if the central bank pays an interest rate on that bond that is higher than the interest rate it receives on its foreign exchange reserves, there is a "sterilization cost."

It may not pay for countries to worry too much about sterilization costs. If the accumulation of reserves can help companies borrow responsibly from international markets at relatively low rates, then the sterilization costs borne by the public sector might be offset by the benefits of cheaper borrowing for the private sector.

A better reason to worry about the cost of accumulating reserves is the opportunity cost of having too many of them. Reserves are, of course, a form of savings. The opportunity cost of saving too much is the forgone welfare-enhancing effects of all the spending that wasn't made. For example, let's say there are "excess" reserves on the balance sheet of developing countries, and let's define that excess as the stock of reserves that is greater than two times the stock of short-term external debt. Using these parameters, the excess in reserves amounted to roughly $2.2 trillion at the end of 2016. If that money had been invested in infrastructure projects with a rate of return of 5 percent, the gain would have been $112 billion per year, or around 0.4 percent of these countries' GDP. Insurance is expensive.[42]

This chapter has sought to explain the rise in capital flows to emerging markets as the consequence of two big forces. The first was the implementation of the "pure" Washington Consensus, which inserted developing countries into the global economy and allowed them to attract substantial flows of largely healthy FDI. The second was the way in which developing countries responded to the "impure" Washington Consensus, which pushed more volatile forms of capital toward them, by insulating themselves against the damage that such volatility could do. Paradoxically, this effort at self-insurance helped make developing countries more attractive than ever before in the eyes of international finance.

But this account leaves one gaping hole, the growing role of China. In the years following China's accession to the World Trade Organization in 2001, China's growth and its increasing weight in the global economy had a transformative effect on other developing countries. The growing influence of China, as well as the implications for the future of the relationship between developing countries and international finance, is what the rest of this book addresses.

FOUR

Thank You, China!

SÃO PAULO, 2002

One question above all occupied the minds of international investors during the middle months of 2002: would Brazil be the next emerging market domino to fall?

Much evidence pointed that way. Starting in the second week of March, an astonishing collapse had taken place in the value of the country's financial assets. The risk premium on Brazil's sovereign debt—its spread over the yield on U.S. Treasury bonds—rose from 700 basis points on March 15 to a peak of 2,450 basis points in late September, implying a probability of around 80 percent that Brazil would default on its external debt during the next five years. The prevailing anxiety among investors was molded by a sense of the apparently endless succession of emerging markets financial crises. The previous five years, after all, had seen financial collapse ricochet from one developing country to another in a way that was beginning to feel inevitable. Just as Argentina's default of December 2001 had been partly triggered by Brazil's 1999 devaluation, it seemed reasonable to think that a debt crisis in Brazil could be triggered in return by an economic meltdown in a large neighboring country that was both Brazil's customer and competitor. Not only had Argentina's imports from Brazil fallen to their lowest levels in ten years but the sudden competitiveness of the Argentine peso posed a strategic threat to Brazilian exports globally. And Argentina was a country in which Brazil's foreign creditors had recently lost a lot of money. By the logic of contagion—both economic and financial—Brazil looked like it was in trouble.

The country seemed to be at risk of a self-fulfilling debt crisis: if enough investors believed that Brazil would default, then their collective rush for the exits might deny the country sufficient funding to prevent a crisis. The daily descent in the value of the Brazilian real, which weakened from 2.3 against the dollar in mid-March to 3.9 in early October, provided a highly visible reminder of how close to the edge Brazil was. Since nearly half the government's debt was either denominated in dollars or linked to the dollar exchange rate, every decline in the real's value pushed up the public debt burden, made a debt crisis more likely, and, with perfect circularity, gave investors another reason to sell the real and buy dollars. This was despite the IMF's decision in early August to lend Brazil $30 billion, its largest-ever loan at the time.

The country's trauma during 2002 wasn't just the product of Argentinian contagion, though. Two unconnected developments had helped to reinforce the sense of panic. The first was the beginning of a sharp fall in the U.S. equity market. From a peak of over 10,600 on March 15, the Dow Jones Industrial Average led a six-month descent in world stock prices that would return the market to levels unseen since the summer of 1998, when the U.S. hedge fund Long-Term Capital Management had been brought down by the aftermath of the Russia crisis. This created an environment that was bound to be uncomfortable for risky borrowers such as Brazil. The second development was the candidacy of Luiz Inácio Lula da Silva, universally known as Lula, in the Brazilian presidential election of October 2002. At the same time that global stock markets were tumbling, opinion polls were beginning to suggest that Lula would be heading for the Planalto, Brazil's presidential palace.

Lula, a metalworker without formal education born to illiterate parents, had become a trade unionist in the 1960s and had helped found Brazil's Workers' Party, the Partido dos Trabalhadores (or PT) in 1980. The 2002 election was his fourth attempt to gain the presidency. Although he had swapped his jeans for a suit during the early stages of the campaign, the market had reason to be nervous. It wasn't just that Lula was not part of

Brazil's traditional governing elite; he was its antithesis. The PT's program, published in December 2001, spoke of "breaking with the current economic model, which is based on opening the market and radical deregulation, and the consequent subordination of the dynamic of the national economic to the interests and whims of global financial capital."[1] The program promised a return to a 1960s world of import substitution behind high tariff walls; a significant expansion of the role of the state; an abandonment of the country's agreement with the IMF, which had been renewed in September 2001; and a renegotiation of the government's external debt. In other words, the entire legacy of the outgoing two-term president, Fernando Henrique Cardoso, would be upended; the Washington Consensus would be ditched.

As it turned out, Lula duly won the election in October 2002 and Brazil avoided default: the panic of the summer subsided almost as quickly as it had begun. Indeed, if you had bought Brazilian bonds in September 2002 and held on to them until the end of 2016, your average annual return would have been close to 11 percent, a yield higher than that on almost any other bond in the emerging markets universe. During the same period, the average annual return on a U.S. Treasury bond was a mere 4.5 percent.

This Brazilian default-that-never-was can be regarded as the end of a chapter of crises that had started in Poland twenty-one years previously. To explain why Brazil avoided a more chaotic end in 2002, it is worth drawing attention to four factors. The first is Lula himself. By the summer of that year, the candidate was distancing himself from the party's published program and had publicly committed himself to adopting a conventional economic framework and to honoring the country's loan agreement with the IMF. In other words, Brazil stepped back from abandoning the globalization project. The second was the fact the Brazilian real had become astonishingly cheap, given the battering it had received both in 1999 and again in 2002. Aside from the Argentine peso and the Indonesian rupiah, almost no other developing country's currency had lost as much value as the real in the previous eight years. This helped shrink Brazil's financing needs by making the country's current account deficit disappear: by late 2002 Brazil was running a surplus on its current account, in contrast to the annualized deficit of almost 5 percent of GDP that it had had to finance in early 2001. The third factor was U.S. monetary policy: by late 2002 the inflation-adjusted federal funds rate was once again negative, for the first time since mid-1993 when capital flows to emerging markets were in their pre-Tequila boom phase. As we've already discovered, negative real U.S. interest rates tend to push capital toward developing countries rather than suck capital from them.

The final factor that saved Brazil in 2002 was China; and China's impact on the developing world is the theme of this chapter. The 2000s saw the beginning of an economic relationship between China and the rest of the developing world that was nothing short of transformational. For generations, developing countries had needed only to look to the United States to get a sense of what economic shocks, positive or negative, they might be subject to. The 2000s changed all that. The clearest manifestation of that change was that decade's extraordinary surge in commodity prices, and it is with an examination of the creation of a "China commodities complex" that we start the analysis. Chinese demand for commodities helped save Brazil, and plenty of other countries, too. Later in this chapter we'll broaden things out to see how China affected developing countries whose economic base lay in the export of manufactured goods rather than commodities.

Commodity Prices Go Boom

By 2002, world commodity prices were in the early stages of a boom the like of which hadn't been seen in centuries. The boom lasted until 2011, well after the shocks created by the global financial crisis that exploded in 2008. Any explanation of this boom must have China at its center.

Commodity prices had been falling almost unremittingly since the early 1980s, a fact that shouldn't be disconnected from the near-perpetual state of crisis in which developing countries found themselves during these years. By 1999 the "average" commodity price was, in inflation-adjusted terms, around 60 percent lower than it had been during the 1979–81 peak, which coincided with the second oil shock. Yet in the years following 1999, real commodity prices rose in an almost uninterrupted fashion.

While there are plenty of different ways of measuring real commodity prices, it is difficult to escape the conclusion that this boom was unique. According to an analysis by Carmen Reinhart and colleagues, the commodity boom that ended in 2011 was the second-longest rise in real commodity prices since the late eighteenth century.[2] Their work suggests that the only commodity boom (for which there are data) that competes with the boom of the 2000s was a thirteen-year boom that lasted from 1938 to 1951. But the China-led boom of the early twenty-first century was only one year shorter than that of the mid-twentieth century, with prices in the recent boom rising by much more. By 2011, an unweighted average of forty real commodity prices was 140 percent higher than it had been in 1999.[3] During the mid-twentieth-century boom, prices increased much more modestly, rising by only 30 percent or so. So it is certainly reasonable to claim that this was probably the biggest peacetime rise in commodity prices for at least 200 years.

China's hand in causing this boom is visible almost anywhere one looks. Between 1995 and 2011, China by itself accounted for almost the entire global increase in demand for zinc, nickel, lead, copper, and tin, and for over a third of the increase in the world's demand for oil. By 2011, when the boom ended, China was consuming 43 percent of the world's output of base metals, about 20 percent of its nonrenewable energy resources, and about 24 percent of major agricultural crops and foodstuffs, including soybeans, beef, corn, wheat, and coffee.[4]

In 1998, Brazil and China each accounted for 3 percent of global GDP, calculated at market prices. By 2011, China's share had reached 10 percent; Brazil's was 4 percent. (By 2015, China's share had risen yet further, to 15 percent, while Brazil's had slipped back to 3 percent.) So the simplest observation one can make is that China's economy grew fast—by an average of 10 percent annually between 1998 and 2011—and kept growing. The result was China's graduation from the status of an important but still rather small developing country—in strict terms of GDP, at least—into that of a global giant. Although China is *of* the developing world, it now shapes the world of which it is a part. It is the first time that the economic life of developing countries has been determined by one of their own.

The Joys of China Dependence

China's oversized status in global commodity markets created a surge in the dependence of commodity exporters on China: their economic fate became intimately connected with China's appetite for basic materials. In 2001, for example, Chile's exports to China were equivalent to a little over 1 percent of Chilean GDP; ten years later, those exports were worth 8 percent of Chilean GDP. Zambia, like Chile a copper producer, saw an exceptional increase in this form of China dependence: Zambia's exports to China rose from practically nothing in 2001 to around 8 percent of the former's GDP in 2011. Brazil, Peru, South Africa, Angola, Russia, and plenty of others enjoyed a similar rise in this form of China dependence.

China dependence had some very happy effects on economic performance for commodity-exporting developing countries. One way of considering this is to look at the growth differential between developing countries and the advanced economies. For commodity exporters in the developing world, the boom years of the 2000s saw GDP growth rates rise 2.1 percentage points above the growth rates of rich countries, a bigger differential than they had enjoyed for generations. In the 1970s that growth differential had been 1.6 percentage points; in the 1980s it had been -1.3 percentage points, and in the 1990s only 0.5 percentage points.

The acceleration in GDP growth supported an improvement in government revenues that, in some countries at least, made room for proper efforts to combat poverty. The most famous of these was Bolsa Família in Brazil, a monthly cash transfer to mothers in low-income families, delivered on the condition that they could prove they were sending their children to school and getting their health checked. The payments were small but ended up reaching more than 12 million households, or a quarter of the population. And the program's effect on reducing poverty was achieved without any sacrifice of financial stability: Brazil's public debt burden fell steadily during the 2000s, from 55 percent of GDP in 2002 to 36 percent in 2011. Thanks to China—at least in part—Brazil under Lula seemed to have been able to spend more and balance its books at the same time. His predecessor, Fernando Henrique Cardoso, had also increased public spending in an attempt to reduce poverty. But unlike Lula, Cardoso oversaw a sharp rise in Brazil's public debt burden, from the 30 percent of GDP level it had been at in 1994 when he was elected. No wonder Lula finished his two terms in office at the end of 2010 with an 80 percent approval rating. China made him lucky.

The big improvement in the terms of trade for commodity-exporting developing countries didn't just bring the economic benefits of accelerating GDP growth and the space that this created for the alleviation of poverty. It also had a particular set of consequences for these countries' relationship with international finance, helping to deliver extraordinary improvements in their balance sheets, well beyond the fall in Brazil's public debt/GDP ratio just mentioned. And since the need to embark on a project of balance sheet improvement was the overwhelming lesson of the era of crises discussed in the previous chapter, it is sensible to conclude that one of China's gifts to the developing world was to make it easier for other developing countries to build financial safety nets.

To understand how China helped to make it possible for countries to increase their financial resilience, let's begin with the effect of the commodities boom on the current account balances of commodity-exporting countries. The starting point for these countries was the experience of years of persistent current account deficits. Indeed, between 1975 and 1998, there was not a single year in which commodity-exporting developing countries—taken as a whole—ran a current account surplus.[5] Yet in the thirteen years from 1999, the very beginning of the commodities boom, until 2011, when the boom ended, there was only one year, 2010, in which these countries produced an aggregate current account deficit.

These surpluses played a critical role in boosting the sovereign creditworthiness of commodity-exporting developing countries. This happened because of both something to do with flows and something to do with stocks. The current account surplus represents a net flow of foreign exchange into an economy. Since that flow reduces a country's external financing needs, market participants tend to reward a country with a current account surplus with lower borrowing costs. And since the current account surplus helps a country build up its foreign exchange reserves, that increase in its stock of foreign assets also supports sovereign creditworthiness.

And certainly these changes in flows and stocks helped support a rise in the creditworthiness of commodity exporters, which collectively saw their sovereign credit ratings improve much more during the commodities boom than was the case for other developing countries. The average sovereign credit rating, according to the Standard & Poor's agency, of a sample of commodity-exporting countries rose by four notches, from a rating of B+ in 2002 to a rating of BBB– in 2011. The significance of this is that a rating of BBB– or its equivalent is what the agencies call "investment grade," implying that a country has adequate capacity to repay its foreign currency–denominated debt. The positive shocks to the terms of trade of commodity-exporting countries were, rightly or wrongly, thought to add up to a permanent improvement in their ability to pay their way in the international financial system.

This improvement in sovereign creditworthiness helped deliver an amazing decline in countries' borrowing costs. At the height of the 2002 panic in Brazil, the average risk premium over U.S. Treasury bond yields for commodity-exporting developing countries was around 1,000 basis points higher than the risk premium for exporters of manufactured goods. In early 2012, commodity exporters on average paid only 20 basis points more to borrow than did exporters of manufactured goods.

However, it would be wrong to think that the benign shadow that China cast over the economic life of developing countries was limited to commodity exporters. There were two other ways in which emerging economies of varying types became "China shaped" during the 2000s.

The first reflected the fact that a boom in commodity prices supports capital flows to *all* developing countries, regardless of whether they are exporters or importers of commodities. In this respect, the commodities boom of the 2000s was similar to the narrower, oil-driven boom of the 1970s.

Why is it that rising commodity prices support capital flows to all developing countries? The reason is that surges in commodity prices tend to be associated with a positive liquidity shock. We have seen, for example, how the sudden creation of petrodollars in the 1970s meant that a new pool of financing became available that made its way to "risky" borrowers in the developing world. A similar process was at work in the 2000s: as we'll discover a little later in this chapter, oil exporters were also an important source of global liquidity during this decade. Another reason why commodity booms tend to push capital toward developing countries has to do with the coincidence of rising commodity prices and accelerating global growth. In the 2000s, as in the 1970s, growth rates were strong, and so a link could establish itself in the minds of international investors between rising commodity prices and optimism about an increase in global incomes.

As a result of all this, there is a fairly persistent relationship between higher commodity prices and risk appetite among international investors, who become more willing to lend. Because of that relationship, commodity importers may lose out on the *current* account of their balance of payments when commodity prices rise, but they can gain on the *capital* account because the combination of high commodity prices and a strong risk appetite helps deliver capital inflows to these countries. So even if a China-led commodities boom raised the import bill of commodity-importing countries, it also helped provide them with the means to finance that bigger import bill. All in all, it is difficult to identify developing countries that categorically lost out from the creation of the "China commodities complex." (Mexico is probably the best example: after China's accession to the World Trade Organization in 2001, the growth of China's market share in supplying manufactured goods to the United States arguably came at the expense of firms in Mexico more than in any other country.)

The second way in which commodity-importing developing countries became China shaped in the 2000s was that China established a key role for itself in a new global order for trade in manufactured goods, a new order that had begun to evolve in the 1990s. During that decade, a combination of falling tariffs, technological developments in containerization, the arrival of the internet, and the boost in the effective global supply of labor meant that the production of manufactured goods became geographically fragmented. Parts and components started to bounce between countries, at each stage having some value added to them, until they arrived at a location—China, more often than not—where they were assembled into a final product.

So China became a central node in a network of interlinked economies that began to dominate trade in manufactured goods—a network that would help propel China to become, by 2014, the world's biggest manufacturer and its biggest exporter. The countries to which China was connected in these networks were overwhelmingly in Asia. The growth of these "global value chains" meant that during the 1990s and 2000s, trade within the Asian region grew faster than in any other region of the world: by 2010 the fifteen countries in the East Asian region were only slightly less integrated in their trade than the members of the EU.[6]

And just as China's role in global commodity markets created China dependence for such countries as Chile, Brazil, and South Africa, so China's role in global manufacturing created China dependence in such countries as Korea, Taiwan, Singapore, Vietnam, Malaysia, and Thailand. In 2000, Malaysia's exports to China accounted for around 3 percent of Malaysian GDP, but by 2011 this share had risen to 11 percent. Korea's exports saw a similar jump. Thailand's exports to China rose from the equivalent of 2 percent to 7 percent of Thai GDP during the same period.

The China dependence of these manufacturing economies, like the China dependence of the commodity exporters, helped them enjoy GDP growth rates that exceeded rich-country growth rates by a lot more than had been the case during previous decades. For the whole of the 2000s, the gap between the GDP growth rate of manufacturing exporters in the developing world and that of the advanced economies was 5.1 percentage points: these countries grew at an average rate of 6.6 percent, while the rich world grew at an average rate of 1.5 percent. During the peak years of 2002–07—that is to say, after the 2001 global recession and before the worldwide financial crisis—the growth differential was 5.3 percentage points. The developing world's exporters of manufactured goods had never seen anything like this kind of catch-up: in the three decades before 2000, the growth differential had averaged a mere 3.8 percentage points.

And just like its commodity exporters, the developing world's manufacturing exporters used this era of China dependence to transform their current account balances. In the previous chapter we discussed the emergence of current account surpluses as a kind of posttraumatic response to the legacy of the crises of the 1990s: these were the surpluses needed to finance the building of the foreign exchange reserves that helped provide protection against the volatility of global capital flows, and they were the surpluses that resulted from efforts to keep currencies cheap. Now we have a clearer picture of how these surpluses were made possible: it was, to a large degree, thanks to China.

China, in summary, played an indispensable role during the 2000s in creating what might be called an "age of convergence," a period in which developing countries caught up economically with their rich-country counterparts to an extent that had not been achieved in previous episodes of globalization. But it wasn't merely income convergence that China offered. It was income convergence accompanied by current account surpluses that could be used to help finance the establishment of ever-larger financial safety nets. These two features of China's contribution to the developing world made the 2000s truly unique.

The Washington Consensus Meets Its Perfect Student

What did China do to establish such an unambiguous role in shaping the economic life of developing countries? The answer, in a nutshell, is that it adopted aspects of the Washington Consensus, or at least aspects of the "pure" version originally articulated by John Williamson. That shouldn't come as a surprise. After all, the Washington Consensus itself had originally taken some inspiration from the successful outward-looking policy experiments in other Asian countries, such as Korea and Taiwan.

Of course, a careful examination of the list of policies recommended in the Washington Consensus will turn up elements from which China kept its distance: the 1990s and 2000s didn't see much from Beijing in the way of privatization, for example. Interest rate liberalization, another feature of the original Washington Consensus, was also not a priority for Beijing until much later, and the Chinese government's commitment to deregulation and to extending property rights has been rather selective. But it should be kept in mind that in essence, the Washington Consensus was a strategy to push developing countries into a newly globalizing world economy. In its pure form, the strategy was to rely on promoting FDI as a source of capital, keeping other, more volatile forms of capital at bay, and adopting an exchange rate "sufficiently competitive to induce a rapid growth in non-traditional exports." What made developing countries susceptible to financial crisis during the 1990s resulted largely from the "impurities" that came to pervade the original Washington Consensus: an obsession with capital account liberalization and a tolerance of uncompetitive exchange rates in the name of controlling inflation.

China avoided these traps. Its economic strategy was resolutely investment-driven, export-oriented, and FDI-funded, and its renminbi policy complemented this goal by ensuring that the central bank resisted appreciation of the real exchange rate. Though this was the "pure" form of the Washington Consensus, it was implemented with Chinese characteristics. And the result was that China's exports as a share of its GDP rose from around 8 percent in the early 1980s to 35 percent in 2007.

Investment spending, a critical engine of sustainable growth in any economist's model, had already been high in the earliest days of China's economic transition under Deng Xiaoping, and hovered at a level around

30 percent of GDP during the 1980s. In the years that followed, though, a number of shocks occurred that helped increase the economy's reliance on investment spending, so that by 2011 the share of investment in GDP was close to 50 percent. Among these shocks were, first, Deng's "Speech in the South" in 1992, which fortified China's commitment to accelerated economic reform; second, a round of reforms to state-owned enterprises in the late 1990s, which boosted the (investment-oriented) output of those firms; and third, China's accession to the World Trade Organization in 2001, which stimulated investment in export-oriented capacity. A fourth positive shock to China's investment dependence was the government's response to the financial crisis following the collapse of the U.S. investment bank Lehman Brothers in late 2008, a response discussed below. To put all this into context, investment as a share of GDP in the G7 advanced economies was 20 percent in 2011.

From the point of view of commodity exporters such as Brazil, this reliance on investment spending was particularly important because investment-led development, almost by definition, tends to absorb more commodities than a development model driven by consumer spending. In 2010, for example, China's per capita GDP was roughly what Brazil and Korea had enjoyed in the mid-1970s, yet China was using three times as much energy as those economies had when their incomes had been at a similar level.[7]

And the resources available to support this export-oriented, investment-led strategy were consistently augmented by FDI. In a way, this made China unique. Although economists often like to compare China's emergence in the 1980s and 1990s to that of Japan and Korea in earlier decades, one difference stands out: FDI was barely visible in the postwar economic development of Japan and Korea. That was just a fluke of timing: China's economic modernization has coincided with an era of financial globalization in which cross-border flows of FDI have been available. That wasn't the case in the 1950s and 1960s when Japan and Korea first embarked on their own projects of economic renewal.

China's use of FDI inflows was extensive, and was determinedly export-oriented. The connection between investment spending and exports is evident, for example, in the vast expansion of China's port network: by 2013, Shanghai had replaced Singapore as the world's largest port, and five other

Chinese ports ranked in the world's top ten.[8] The link between FDI and exports was also tightened by fiscal incentives, which exempted imports from tariffs or value-added taxes as long as they were used as inputs for the export sector. Indeed, the preferential tax treatment of foreign investment compared to domestic investment led to "round-tripping," or the surreptitious conversion of a domestic investment into a foreign one: that's why Hong Kong was for many years the biggest source of FDI inflows to China. Another example of these tax benefits was the corporate tax discount offered to foreign firms in China whose exports accounted for more than 70 percent of their turnover.[9]

Between 1986 and 2005, FDI flows into China amounted on average to the equivalent of nearly 3 percent of the country's GDP, though the surge of these inflows properly began only in 1993, the year after Deng's southern tour. By 2005, 58 percent of China's exports were sold by foreign-owned firms.[10]

Normally, one might worry that a capital inflow this large sustained over a lengthy period might lead to an appreciation of the exchange rate. Not so in China, whose exchange rate policy was as carefully honed to support exports as were its policies on FDI. That meant that the central bank spent a lot of effort intervening in the foreign exchange market to prevent the renminbi from appreciating in nominal terms. And that in turn helped limit its appreciation in real terms. By the end of the 1990s, the real effective exchange rate of the renminbi was no more elevated than it had been at the beginning of the decade—a remarkable show of stability. Or we could consider a broader period: during the twenty years between 1990 and 2009, China's real exchange rate was extraordinarily stable. By 2009 the real effective exchange rate was less than 10 percent stronger than it had been twenty years earlier. The Thai baht and Malaysian ringgit, on the other hand, were around 18 percent stronger in real terms than they were at the start of the 1990s, despite the sharp depreciations they suffered during the course of the 1990s.

China's success in staying competitive by stabilizing its real exchange rate is at least partly due to the effort it made to keep its capital account rather closed: it didn't have to worry about exchange rate pressures coming from large inflows of speculative capital. And here is China's central point of departure from the impure version of the Washington Consensus so beloved by U.S. policymakers and free-market fundamentalists: *Beijing never signed up to the idea that a developing country's capital account should be open to all kinds of inflow.*

As much as it embraced FDI, China also more or less scorned anything that smacked of "hot money." The controls on capital inflows that were in place during the 1990s meant that foreigners had strictly limited access to local capital market instruments in China, and no access at all to money market instruments. Moreover, the ability of Chinese firms to borrow abroad was highly circumscribed: in the mid-1990s, Chinese banks and firms needed approval from the State Administration of Foreign Exchange (SAFE) if they wanted to borrow abroad. For any loan that wasn't obviously financing trade transactions, a prospective borrower needed to prove that any long-term foreign loan it sought was part of the state plan for utilizing foreign capital. Portfolio inflows remained, for all intents and purposes, forbidden until the early 2010s. These restrictions helped ensure that China's external balance sheet was consistently strong. When the Asian crisis hit in 1997, China's total external debt was $120 billion, compared to a stock of foreign exchange reserves of $140 billion. Indeed, there hasn't been a single year since 1981 in which China's foreign debt has been larger than its foreign exchange reserves.

And if China had ever been tempted to follow the advice coming out of Washington during the 1990s regarding the wisdom of capital account liberalization, the events of 1997 put paid to that. China saw clearly the kind of devastation that could be wrought by volatile capital flows. Equally, China was as diligent as any other economy in the region when it came to learning the lessons of the crisis: keep your balance sheet strong by building up foreign exchange reserves.

It is easy to praise China's success in keeping its balance sheet strong, but much less easy to argue that its model could be easily reproduced by other developing countries. The reason for that lies in a unique feature in the structure of China's economy: its exceptionally high rate of savings.

The current account balance for any country is simply the difference between how much it saves and how much it invests. And while China has done an astonishing amount of investing, its savings have regularly exceeded that amount. It is for that reason, above all, that China has been able to maintain its current account surpluses and to fund its accumulation of foreign exchange reserves.

Describing China's savings behavior is easier than explaining it. The central fact is that China's overall savings ratio started high and grew higher: from just below 40 percent of GDP throughout the 1990s to just over 50 percent in the years that followed the global financial crisis. The two dominant sources of savings in China are its households and its firms. For households, high-saving behavior may have some cultural roots, a factor emphasized by Zhou Xiaochuan, until recently the governor of the People's Bank of China, for example,[11] but a number of simple economic developments in China also have helped keep household savings high. One of these was the decision, sustained for many years, to keep interest rates on households' bank deposits low. If households receive little in the way of interest income from their deposit accounts, the natural response is to increase the size of those accounts—to save more, in other words—in order to generate a target level of income. And when corporate restructuring in the 1990s led to the disappearance of the cradle-to-grave social safety net—China's "iron rice bowl"—households also responded by increasing their savings since they could no longer rely on their state-owned employers to provide housing or social benefits.

The savings of China's corporations have also been high and rising during the past twenty-five years. This is merely a reflection of their profitability: industrial profits accounted for just under 2 percent of GDP in the late 1990s, but this share rose to over 10 percent in 2007, the year before the Lehman Brothers crisis. And the profitability of those firms was nicely supported by the fact that a lot of the inputs into China's production processes were kept cheap: land and capital were offered to firms at rates that almost certainly contained subsidies, and labor was cheap, too, partly thanks to the *hukou* system of household registration that denies migrant workers access to the social welfare benefits that their locally born counterparts receive.

A country with high savings is in a truly fortunate position when it comes to the risks of financial instability that are created by international capital. The higher its savings as a share of GDP, the more able it is to finance domestic investment with its own resources, or, to put it another way, the more likely it is to be running a permanent, or structural, current account surplus: it doesn't need the rest of the world's money. Having a high savings/GDP ratio, in other words, permits a pattern of growth that cannot easily be destabilized by a sudden reversal of international finance: you are more or less safe from the herd. For China, that safety was further secured by its policies with respect to its capital account since it sought less volatile FDI flows rather than anything more risky. And in China's case, the benign effects of its exceptionally high savings/GDP ratio weren't just kept to itself; they were shared with other developing countries, too. The next task is to explain why.

Surpluses, and What to Do with Them

China's accumulation of current account surpluses was extraordinary. Just consider the period between 1999 and 2011: the years in which developing countries as a whole were producing a current account surplus. During these years, the accumulated surplus of *all* developing countries was $3 trillion. Some of this, around $0.7 trillion, came from the five countries most traumatized by the Asian crisis: Indonesia, Thailand, Malaysia, the Philippines, and Korea. Another $0.7 trillion of that accumulated surplus came from Russia and the other countries of the former Soviet Union. But during these years China itself racked up an accumulated current account surplus of $1.9 trillion. Almost two-thirds of the whole current account surplus of developing countries during that thirteen-year period, then, came from just one of them.

This era of current account surpluses—which in various ways was the legacy of the trauma of the Asian crisis, the commodities boom, and the export boost that China gave to countries connected to it by global value chains—poses a question: where did all the surpluses go?

The answer is quite straightforward: the developing world's current account surpluses helped build its foreign exchange reserves. For economies that had suffered as a result of the Asian crisis and its contagion effects, this was the whole point of the exercise: surpluses were sought—or were welcomed, at least—precisely for the way they could help build up buffers and reduce vulnerability to sudden changes in direction of international capital flows. The strength of China's external balance was correctly reckoned to be the main reason why China avoided a crisis in 1997. And so it seemed natural to conclude that "copying China"—running current account surpluses and accumulating reserves—was a reliable way of fending off the risk of financial crises in the future.

For China itself, the generation of dollars from its current account surpluses was at the forefront of the reserves-building process. Between 1999 and 2014, China's accumulation of $2.6 trillion in such surpluses funded the bulk of the $3.7 trillion increase in its foreign exchange reserves, which rose from $150 billion at the end of 1998 to nearly $3.9 trillion at the end of 2014.

And what then happened to these reserves? Again, the answer is simple: a large chunk of these reserves was used to buy U.S. Treasury bonds and bills, IOUs that are safe and liquid enough to be considered the world's premier reserve assets. By the end of 2016, developing countries owned $2.7 trillion worth of debt issued by the U.S. Treasury, an increase of $2.3 trillion since 2002. In other words, around 40 percent of the whole increase in developing countries' reserves since 1999 was invested in the U.S. Treasury market. And China, of course, led the way: its ownership of U.S. Treasury debt was $1.2 trillion at the end of 2016.

In making these purchases, developing countries saw their ownership of U.S. government debt double from the equivalent of 5 percent of their GDP to 10 percent. At the peak of this process of accumulation in 2012, developing countries as a whole owned a *quarter* of the entire stock of marketable U.S. government debt.

What was the result of this increase in developing countries' ownership of U.S. public debt? In chapter 3 we discussed a kind of virtuous circle in which the increase in foreign exchange reserves can lead to an increase in capital inflows because of the way a rise in reserves makes a country more creditworthy, and because of the way the accumulation of reserves can help keep a currency from losing competitiveness quickly. In the 2000s, the scale of the increase in reserves, and the way that these new reserves were largely invested in U.S. government bonds, meant that a new kind of virtuous circle began to appear. As developing countries came to own more and more U.S. government debt, this tended to push down the yields on that debt, which in turn made international investors even more interested in buying the higher-yielding debt of developing countries.

In the early chapters of this book, it was explained that capital flows to developing countries can be understood in terms of push factors—the way real U.S. interest rates affect the flow of finance—and pull factors, or the fundamental attractiveness of lending to a country. What we have here is a situation where the pull factor of rising reserves and stronger creditworthiness actually created its own push factor by depressing U.S. yields and therefore pushing more capital toward higher-yielding developing countries. And because China's current account surplus, its stock of reserves, and its ownership of U.S. government debt became such a dominant influence in this process, here is another reason why developing countries might say, "Thank you, China!" There is one more reason: the way China's response to the Lehman Brothers crisis in 2008 prevented a greater catastrophe for the emerging economies that had become so dependent on it.

China's Balance Sheet Comes to the Rescue

Economists often refer to China's growing weight in global GDP—how these days it accounts for some 15 percent of world GDP at market exchange rates, up from only 2 percent in the early 1990s, and how the country has established itself as the world's second-largest economy after the United States (which accounts for around 25 percent of world GDP). A more revealing indicator, though, is China's contribution to global GDP *growth*. On this measure, the phenomenon of China dependence comes into sharper focus. In 1990, China was responsible for only 2 percent of global GDP growth. In the years between 2010 and 2013, though, China's contribution to global GDP growth averaged 30 percent, precisely twice the contribution of the United States.

How China established this exceptional importance in generating global GDP growth boils down to its response to the global financial crisis. While the developed world was sucked into its worst crisis since the 1930s, China used the strength of its balance sheet to boost its domestic spending and keep economic activity buoyant. All it had to suffer was the pain of real GDP growth falling from just over 14 percent in 2007 to just below 10 percent in the following two years.

The headline of this stimulus was a fiscal package worth $586 billion, equal to around 12 percent of China's GDP in 2008. But the real meat of the stimulus was quasi-fiscal: "quasi" in the sense that state-owned Chinese banks vastly increased their lending to local governments, which then spent the proceeds on an infrastructure-led investment spree. As a result, in the three years between 2008 and 2011, the amount of outstanding credit in China rose from 122 percent of GDP to 167 percent.

Beijing's ability to stabilize its economy in the wake of the global crisis helped to prevent the crisis turning into a catastrophe for China-dependent emerging economies. That's not to say that these countries sailed through the aftermath of the collapse of Lehman Brothers. In 2009, developing countries' growth slowed to its lowest rate in decades, and some countries—Ukraine and the Baltic states, for example—suffered huge economic collapses, thanks to precrisis credit splurges that had been considered safe because of their largely foreign-owned banking systems. Russia suffered a capital outflow so large during late 2008 that it lost over a third of its foreign exchange reserves in six months.

But the shock was brief. China's stimulus was a gift: it provided a welcome new source of global demand when developed countries fell into recession. And though net capital flows to developing countries turned negative in 2008, there was no catastrophe: net flows resumed in 2009 to the tune of more than 2 percent of developing countries' GDP.

Of course, China wasn't all that was working in developing countries' favor during the global financial crisis. Two other forces helped keep capital flowing to developing countries and either prevented them from slipping into recession or made the downturn less severe. The first was the fact that emerging economies had come to have exceptionally strong balance sheets. In 2000, only five of fifty emerging economies had foreign exchange reserves that were higher than the external debt owed by their governments; in other words, there were only five that could be described as net external creditors. By 2007 that number had risen to twenty-five. Indeed, it could reasonably be argued that the accumulation of reserves by developing countries was a partial *cause* of the financial crisis in the North Atlantic: their endless investment of those reserves in the market for U.S. Treasury securities helped to misprice risk globally by pushing down U.S. yields to levels that did not reflect the buildup of vulnerability in the financial system. The second force that helped to keep developing countries afloat was U.S. monetary policy: the Fed's response to the crisis ensured that inflation-adjusted short-term interest rates turned negative once again; that helped push capital toward developing countries, in a way that had become familiar since Cuba's Dance of the Millions.

By 2015, China's contribution to global GDP growth had reached over 40 percent. A debate rages about the sustainability of China's growth, given its dependence on a persistent supply of credit whose efficiency has declined and which may not be fully repaid. Never mind that. What's important for our purposes is the position that China has established in shaping the economic lives of developing countries, a position that now looks like a permanent feature of the global economy.

Two important questions come out of this. The first is whether China will ever be able and willing to translate its *economic* influence over the level of activity in the developing world into *intellectual* influence over the shape of policymaking. As we saw in earlier chapters, in the twentieth century the United States did just that, converting its economic clout into policy advice across the developing world, from the Kemmerer Missions to those of Jeffrey Sachs and the role that the Washington Consensus, in its impure version, played in shaping the kinds of choices that developing countries made in formulating economic policy.

The second question is this: if China ever does aspire to shaping the policy agenda for developing countries, what might that agenda look like? We have already seen how Beijing's approach to policymaking can be described as pure Washington Consensus with Chinese characteristics: a rigorously outward-looking strategy that has entailed encouraging FDI, keeping its currency cheap, eschewing an open capital account, and keeping the state at the center of economic activity. Of course, China's model would have very little chance of being replicated by any other country. Aside from anything else, it is practically impossible to find countries that have anything like the savings ratios of Chinese households and corporations. But it is not complicated to imagine a future in which China's growing role in the economic life of the developing world might change the developing world's relationship to international finance. The next chapter makes some suggestions as to what that kind of future might look like.

FIVE

Toward a Beijing Consensus

BEIJING, 2015

On a clear, cold afternoon in early 2015, I made my way across Beijing to the northwest of the city, where the suburban calm and Qing-era architecture of Peking University offer a welcome escape from the modern capital. I was there to meet Professor Justin Yifu Lin, arguably China's most famous economist and very likely its most influential one. Lin had been the first Chinese student after the Cultural Revolution to return to China with an American doctorate in economics (from the University of Chicago) and had played an important role in guiding the reform process that opened China's economy to the rest of the world, before becoming the chief economist of the World Bank in 2008. What makes him especially unusual is that he is originally from Taiwan. As a twenty-six-year-old army captain stationed on the islands of Quemoy, he defected to the mainland in May 1979 by swimming across the Taiwan Straits. As his life's goal had been to "make the Chinese prosperous," he came to the conclusion that he could make a larger contribution by attaching himself to the more populous part of the Chinese nation.[1]

At the end of our discussion, Professor Lin handed me an article he had written that would shortly be published. It was titled "Why I Do Not Support Full Capital Account Liberalization," and it offers two main arguments. It begins by stressing the distinction between "real" and "financial" capital inflows. The former are essentially equivalent to FDI, and Lin is unequivocally supportive of their contribution to a developing country's growth. The latter are more or less everything else, and about these types of inflows he expresses varying degrees of suspicion. He argues that short-term capital inflows in particular do little to support any increase in productivity and that the volatility of these flows is inconsistent with a developing country's economic stability.

The second argument in the article is a thinly veiled attack on the role that Washington and Wall Street played in promoting capital account liberalization in developing countries in the late twentieth century. Lin says that in the wake of the collapse of the Bretton Woods system in the early 1970s, the United States was the "primary beneficiary" of capital account liberalization in other countries. And its banks were, too. As he puts it, "Wall Street became the most active advocator of capital account liberalization, because investment bankers could engage in large-scale arbitrage overseas."[2] In a strange sort of way, Lin's analysis is similar that of Denis Healey in 1974—with both men unhappy to award privileges to U.S. financial institutions.[3] In any event, Lin offers the prediction that capital account liberalization for China would create a high risk of crisis, and repeatedly warns against it.

Lin's negative assessment of the wisdom of capital account liberalization—for developing countries in general, and for China in particular—is by no means a view from the fringe: it reflects mainstream Chinese thinking about international capital mobility. In 2015 Zhou Xiaochuan, the governor of the People's Bank of China and the technocrat to whom Westerners often ascribed liberalizing instincts, gave a speech in Washington during the spring meetings of the IMF and World Bank. "The capital account convertibility China is seeking to achieve is not based on the traditional concept of being fully or freely convertible," Zhou declared. "Instead, drawing lessons from the global financial crisis, China will adopt a concept of *managed convertibility*" (emphasis added).[4] China's aim, Zhou continued, is to carefully manage the buildup of external debt, and in particular to manage the flow of short-term speculative capital. Full liberalization of capital flows, in other words, is not on China's agenda.

China's views about global capital mobility help define what this chapter describes as an emerging "Beijing Consensus." But a Beijing Consensus includes more than a mere set of ideas about the capital account of the balance of payments. The essential distinction between a Beijing Consensus and the Washington Consensus ultimately has to do with the balance of power between states and markets. If the Washington Consensus emphasized how free markets could support growth by pushing a country toward engagement with a global economy, the emerging Beijing Consensus seems set to emphasize the greater role that the state can play in pursuing that goal.

It is worth pointing out that this way of thinking is not especially Chinese. China's desire to restrict capital mobility is really only a new version of John Williamson's "pure" conception of the Washington Consensus, discussed in chapter 3. And the broader idea of rebalancing the respective roles of the state and the market gives the Beijing Consensus historical roots that stretch back to the pre-1971 consensus about the way the global economy should be shaped. Just as the economic statesmen who convened at Bretton Woods in 1944 devised an international system in which governments would promote growth by restricting capital flows, so China wants its government to regain a role in managing capital flows to achieve the same end.

In light of this, the task of this chapter is to set out the likely contours of a Beijing Consensus, and to ask what chance it has of replacing its Western predecessor. But since China's views about global capital mobility are so central to the debate, this is where we begin.

Managed Convertibility:
Yes to Internationalization, No to Liberalization

On the face of it, it might seem odd for China's central bank governor to express hostility to full capital account openness. After all, the central bank had been moving gradually but consistently in the direction of a more liberalized capital account in previous years: China had begun to allow "qualified" foreign institutional investors to invest in some stock exchanges in 2002, and further steps toward liberalization were taken in the following years, even to the extent of allowing some short-term borrowing from foreign creditors. And in 2017 China was taking steps toward including its government debt in the bond indices against which global investors measure their performance, a move intended to attract international portfolio inflows.

Another reason why managed convertibility might look like a strange objective is that it seems at odds with China's evident desire to make the renminbi a global currency. Indeed, 2015 was the very year in which China took a particularly important step toward that goal: in November, the IMF announced that the renminbi was to become one of the currencies, along with the dollar, euro, yen, and sterling, used by the IMF to underpin its own reserve asset, the special drawing rights, or SDRs. In some informal sense, becoming part of the "SDR basket" would confer on the renminbi the status of a global reserve currency. How can China insist on "managing" the convertibility of its currency and simultaneously aspire to making the renminbi a reserve currency? Surely there is something in the definition of a reserve currency, or global currency, that requires investors to be able to buy and sell it at will?[5]

The answer is that formally, no such requirement exists. What is needed is simply that a currency be "freely usable." This bit of IMF-speak dates back to 1978, a time when the United Kingdom and France had capital controls—and when the prevailing orthodoxy still contained remnants of the Bretton Woods regime, which had relied on restricting global capital movements. Of course, a freely usable currency must have *some* degree of convertibility, but just how much is not set in stone. So, because of a resemblance between the West's pre-Washington Consensus monetary doctrine and the modern Chinese one, the SDR gives the renminbi a path to reserve currency status that sidesteps full convertibility.

By taking that path, China aims to carve out a role for the state that doesn't currently exist in the system of reserve currencies. In effect, China is asserting a distinction between currency *internationalization* and currency *liberalization*: it wants the former much more than it wants the latter. One illustration of how China's thinking has changed is the way its goals regarding the capital account are reflected in official Communist Party documents. In 2012, the "political report" that was delivered at the Eighteenth Party Congress included the goal to "gradually realize capital account convertibility." By 2017, though, officials had decided to drop any reference to capital account opening in the political report to the Nineteenth Party Congress.

What all this amounts to is a desire by Chinese policymakers to put the state, rather than the market, back at the center of decision making about global capital movements. And in place of a rule—"open your capital accounts"—China would like to reassert the value of policymakers' *discretion:* "To these inflows, yes please; to those, no thanks."

China's relatively hostile attitude toward fully open capital accounts was hardened by its experience following the global financial crisis in 2008. The U.S. Federal Reserve's dramatic easing of monetary policy—cutting its interest rate effectively to zero and implementing a program of asset purchases known as quantitative easing—helped push capital to developing countries. A large chunk of that capital flowed to China. In the five years between 2009 and 2014, for example, the amount owed by Chinese borrowers to international banks went up by some $1 trillion, an amount equivalent to around 10 percent of China's GDP in 2014. By any standards, this is a huge amount of external borrowing, but what was truly astounding about China's accumulation of foreign debt during this period was that it was made up almost entirely of short-term debt. Data from the Bank for International Settlements suggest that around 80 percent of the increase in China's foreign indebtedness to banks during that five-year period was made up of loans with maturities of less than a year.

Chinese borrowers, in short, succumbed to the logic of *plata dulce.* During this 2009–14 period, the renminbi was either predictably stable against the U.S. dollar or, starting in early 2010, appreciating steadily. So, like their Argentinian counterparts in the 1970s (or their Asian ones in the 1990s), Chinese banks and firms found it highly convenient to borrow dollars at short maturities, sell the dollars for renminbi, and then invest the renminbi in accounts offering interest rates much higher than the rate at which they were borrowing the dollars. And since the renminbi was strengthening against the dollar for most of this period, Chinese borrowers could also gain from the lower cost of buying dollars when it came time to repay their loans. It was pure speculation: with its persistent current account surplus, China had no underlying economic need to increase its external debt in this way.

In predictable fashion, these capital inflows turned into capital outflows when U.S. monetary policy started to tighten. The first sign of that tightening came in May 2013, when Fed chair Ben Bernanke announced that the U.S. Central Bank would wind down its bond-buying program and tighten monetary policy in a form of tapering. In December 2015, the Fed actually raised its policy rate for the first time since the 2008 crisis. The effect of all this on China's capital account was plain to see from what happened to its stock of foreign exchange reserves: having risen from $2 trillion to $4 trillion between 2009 and the middle of 2014, China's reserves fell to $3 trillion by late 2016. Only tightening regulation by Chinese policymakers to limit capital outflows in the second half of 2016 stopped China's reserves from falling further.

China's current account surplus and overall balance sheet strength—reflecting its status as a significant net creditor to the rest of the world—meant that the country could let these huge amounts of dollars flow out of the country without much in the way of economic dislocation. But the experience was to nudge China further away from any enthusiasm for unfettered global capital mobility. And China wasn't alone.

The Death of Capital Account Fundamentalism

The wave of capital that was pushed toward developing countries by loose U.S. monetary policy after the global financial crisis was met with a revival of interest in capital controls as a way of deterring unwelcome inflows. Brazil, for example, reintroduced its IOF, a financial transactions tax, in October 2009, at a rate of 2 percent for all portfolio inflows, both fixed income and equity. By late October 2010, just after the Brazilian finance minister, Guido Mantega, famously complained that "we're in the midst of an international currency war,"[6] the tax rate had increased to 6 percent, and other measures were announced too: an unremunerated reserve requirement (URR) on banks' foreign exchange liabilities (January 2011) and a tax on foreign borrowing (March 2012).[7]

Brazil was joined in these efforts by other countries. Indonesia announced a six-month holding period on bonds issued by the central bank, to deter short-term speculation by foreigners that would have added unwelcome volatility to its foreign exchange market. Peru levied a 400-basis-point fee on foreigners' purchases of its central bank's paper; again, the point was to deter inflows of footloose foreign capital. Thailand imposed a 15 percent withholding tax on foreigners' income from holding its government's bonds; and Korea restored withholding taxes on interest income and transfer gains from foreigners' investments in bonds issued by the Korean government and central bank.

India's role in this debate is especially worth noting. If China is a poster-child for the idea that a developing country need not open its capital account to enjoy rapid rates of growth, India's face is on the poster, too. In 1992, both countries had levels of per capita GDP that were equal to only 5 percent of that of the United States in purchasing-power-parity terms. By 2016, China's per capita GDP had risen to 27 percent of that of the United States, but India's improvement wasn't all that bad, either: its per capita income in 2016 had more than doubled to 12 percent of that of the United States. India's capital account has opened slowly and reluctantly, and India remains one of the least financially open economies among the group of developing countries that have access to international capital markets.[8] Policymakers in India have traditionally been suspicious of the accumulation of external debt and have been careful to limit the inflow of portfolio investment into the country's bond markets. In late 2017, for example, India was still imposing a ceiling on the total stock of foreign investment in its markets for its central government bonds ($38 billion) and for state government bonds ($5 billion)—minuscule amounts for an economy with a 2017 GDP of some $2.5 trillion. Like China—and like John Williamson—India's preferred form of external financing is FDI, and it has been highly successful in attracting it. In the ten years up to 2016, India's net inflow of FDI amounted to around $385 billion, enough to finance almost two-thirds of the cumulative current account deficit that it generated during those years.

If there is an "Indian view" about capital account liberalization, it is perhaps best expressed in a 2013 paper published by the IMF titled "The International Monetary System: Where Are We and Where Do We Need to Go?"[9] The authors, all senior Indian government officials, worried about the prospect of an endless flow of capital toward developing countries. As long as developing countries have faster growth and higher interest rates than their counterparts in the developed world, the risk will remain that these magnets for capital inflows might lead to unwelcome currency appreciation, credit surges, and booms in local asset prices—all contributing to the risk of "a severe crisis down the line."[10] Their conclusion is that capital controls should be an acceptable part of a developing country's toolkit and that "the notion that capital account management measures should be temporary, or a last recourse, is flawed."[11]

India's enthusiasm for controlling capital flows is echoed by others, including the governor of the Malaysian central bank, who concluded that capital controls can be a necessary tool to avoid excessive inflows: "Some would argue that having deeper financial markets would allow EMEs [emerging market economies] to better absorb these capital inflows. This may or may not be the case. It is not easy for EMEs to develop such deep markets and, even if they do, deeper financial markets are a double-edged sword. While the availability of more instruments and participants may mitigate the extreme volatility seen in shallow markets, it may also be the case that the availability of deep and liquid markets may end up attracting more capital inflows."[12]

These sorts of views, as expressed by policymakers in China, India, and Malaysia, are increasingly backed by intellectual and institutional support from elsewhere. The intellectual support comes from what's called the "new economics of capital controls." The argument here is that there is an analogy between external financing and pollution: just as it suits a driver to enjoy his mobility without worrying about the effect he is having on the environment, so it suits an investor to manage his portfolio without worrying about his contribution to global financial fragility. And just as it makes sense to tax polluters, so it makes sense to tax capital flows, because "external financing "pollutes" emerging economies with financial fragility."[13]

The institutional support for greater control of capital flows has come from none other than the IMF itself. In November 2012 the Fund published an "institutional view" of the liberalization and management of capital flows. The document illustrates the distance that Washington has traveled since the 1990s, when Stanley Fischer and his boss, Michel Camdessus, were arguing in favor of giving the IMF a mandate to push the world toward fully open capital accounts (see chapter 3).

To be sure, the document offers little to suggest that the IMF has lost its basic enthusiasm for capital account liberalization. As it says, "Capital flows can enhance the efficiency of resource allocation and the competitiveness of the financial sector." But the meat of the document is its statement that "there is no presumption that full liberalization is an appropriate goal for all countries at all times." The IMF, in other words, has accepted in principle the possibility of a world where restrictions on capital movements can healthily remain part of the structure of international finance. And the IMF expresses clearly its more tolerant approach to the use of capital controls—

now more politely called capital flow management measures, or CFMs—as tools to allow countries to manage sudden changes in the flow of capital across borders. Its only recommendations are that these measures should be temporary, shouldn't be a substitute for responsible economic policies, and shouldn't rattle the confidence of investors.[14]

What we seem to have here is a growing body of evidence—a change of heart at the IMF; China, India, and others unconvinced of the merits of fully liberalized capital flows; and a persistent interest in the use of capital controls by several developing countries—that seems to point to the idea that we are now in a world in which capital account fundamentalism is dead. There is barely an influential voice in international finance now making the case that more capital mobility is undeniably better.

But identifying a problem is often simpler than pointing to the solution. Policymakers in developing countries might well be unhappy about global capital mobility, but that doesn't necessarily lead to the conclusion that using capital controls makes sense. For one, there is a largely unresolved question about whether capital controls actually work. Most economists acknowledge that, in the end, "money will find a way": in other words, if firms or citizens really want to get funds into or out of a country, their ingenuity in discovering new ways to do so will tend to exceed the ingenuity of policymakers in stopping them. The mouse is nimbler than the cat. And it is also quite coherent to argue that by introducing a barrier between a country's financial markets and those of the rest of the world, capital controls can allow governments to get away with undisciplined management of public finances and allow a country's banks to misprice capital domestically. When all is said and done, capital controls might not work even if they were desirable and might not be desirable even if they worked.

And there are two further problems. The first of these is that not all countries are equally free to consider controls on capital inflows or outflows: some countries just have too little in the way of domestic savings to be able to finance the level of investment needed to support GDP growth. Low levels of savings tend to accompany low levels of investment, and that means scant optimism about raising per capita GDP without the help of foreign savings. That trap can be escaped only by relying on external financing to allow domestic investment spending to exceed the capacity of domestic savings to fund it. That in turn means running a current account deficit, with all the vulnerabilities that this can entail if it means a country exposing itself to the volatility of global capital flows. And if low savings lock a country into a dependence on the "kindness of strangers," irritating those strangers with capital controls might not be a strategy that many countries will find attractive.

China and India have had enviable track records in generating rapid growth and impressive declines in poverty without opening their economies up to unfettered flows of global capital. However, keeping their capital accounts relatively closed has been an affordable luxury for them: both countries have high levels of domestic saving. During the twenty years between 1996 and 2015, the share of China's GDP that was saved averaged 46 percent each year; India's share was 33 percent on average. High savings ratios such as these liberate a country from any structural dependence on external financing. And it is not even the case that having a high savings ratio eliminates the need to run a current account deficit. India has tended to run a current account deficit; China hasn't. But high savings ratios do give a country's policymakers freedom to maneuver when it comes to thinking about how to manage their capital account.

Unfortunately, there is no easy path to raising a country's savings rate to a high enough level to provide this kind of freedom. In the first place, the bulk of the evidence seems to suggest that savings ratios rise over time only because of economic growth, rather than because there is some clear set of policies that can boost a country's savings rate. Growth drives savings, in other words, and not the other way around. In the early 1970s, for example, East Asian savings ratios were lower than Latin America's: it was only the rapid growth of East Asian economies over the next decades that boosted their domestic savings.[15] And even for countries that grow, savings ratios tend to be sticky: only a minority of countries can easily graduate from being low-savings economies to high-savings ones.

Another problem with the idea that developing countries will leap to impose capital controls, should such measures become fully accepted, comes from the argument that the efforts by developing countries to "wrap up warmly," or insulate themselves against market volatility, during the past twenty years have made capital controls redundant. The whole point of controlling capital flows is to reduce the risk of a financial crisis. But it is becoming tempting to claim that developing countries seem to have become, in a sense, crisis-proof. And if that's the case, the argument for controls on capital flows might have been weakened.

The "Crisis-proofing" of Emerging Markets?

In what sense is it possible to make the seemingly bold claim that emerging economies have become crisis-proof? The answer lies in the shocks to which these countries were subject between 2012 and 2015. During these years, developing countries were the victims of three nasty surprises. The first was the fall in commodity prices following a boom that, as discussed in chapter 4, probably constituted the most significant peacetime rise in commodity prices during the past two centuries. The peak in global commodity prices occurred during the summer of 2011, after which a gradual fall was evident. That gradual fall turned into something more chaotic during the second half of 2014, when the price of oil, for example, fell from $110 per barrel in June to below $50 per barrel by the end of the year. Just as the rise in commodity prices had supported developing countries, the fall in prices was a blow.

A second shock, not unrelated to the first, to which developing countries were subject during these years was a dramatic decline in the growth of global trade. To put that collapse into some context, it is worth bearing in mind that for almost the entire period after World War II, global trade volumes grew at a faster rate than real global GDP. That differential peaked in the 1990s, when global trade volumes grew at an average rate each year of 6.5 percent, while global GDP grew on average by 2.7 percent a year. The differential between trade growth and GDP growth was almost as large in the 2000s, at least until the global financial crisis. But during the four years between 2012 and 2015, the growth rate of trade volumes suffered a shocking fall and was actually below the growth rate of global GDP. This was a collapse in trade the like of which the world hadn't seen in seventy-odd years. Since trade growth is supposed to support GDP growth, collapsing trade is unlikely to bode well for developing countries' ability to lift income levels for their citizens.

The last of the three shocks to hit developing countries during these years was the Fed's gradual move away from the extremely loose monetary policy with which it had responded to the global financial crisis. This shift started with an announcement by the Fed in May 2013 that it was only a few months away from beginning to scale back the bond buying that had been at the center of its quantitative easing strategy.

It was this final shock that had the most visible consequence for developing countries, in the form of the "taper tantrum" of mid-2013, a rapid capital outflow concentrated on a group of countries that quickly became known as the "Fragile Five": Turkey, South Africa, Brazil, Indonesia, and India. What was common to these countries was that their current account deficits had grown substantially in the years following 2009. In Turkey, for example, a current account deficit of only 1.8 percent of GDP in 2009 had grown to one of 6.7 percent of GDP by 2013. In Turkey, Brazil, Indonesia, and India, there had also been a rapid rise in the external debt of companies. In Brazil, for example, the total debt owed to banks abroad doubled between early 2009 and early 2012, from $93 billion to $186 billion.

In the face of these shocks, currencies weakened, interest rates went up, foreign reserves declined, and economic growth slowed. The Indonesian rupiah weakened sharply, from just under 9,800 to the dollar in May 2013 to over 12,200 by January 2014; the South African rand fell from 9.4 to the dollar to just over 11.1 during those same months. And during the whole of this unpleasant period, 2012 to 2015, the Russian ruble and the Brazilian real each fell by around 40 percent in inflation-adjusted terms. Currency depreciation on this scale is something one usually associates with a financial crisis: in the twelve months after Argentina's 2001 crisis, for example, its exchange rate fell by some 50 percent in real terms. And the effect of these shocks on growth was miserable. Brazil, for example, suffered its deepest and longest recession on record: by late 2016, when the recession ended, Brazilian GDP was almost 9 percent lower in real terms than it had been in early 2014. Russia and South Africa, too, fell into recession. In Russia's case, the two-year recession in 2015 and 2016 was longer than the one that had followed its 1998 default.

Extraordinarily, none of these shocks produced messy defaults or banking sector meltdowns, or necessitated widespread involvement of the IMF. True, the IMF did become a bit more active in those years—emergency lending programs were agreed to with Ukraine, Jamaica, Sri Lanka, and Egypt, among others—but the fund didn't seem to be driving an ambulance throughout the developing world, as it did in the 1980s and 1990s, in order to administer first aid to crisis-hit countries.

To explain why the shocks of 2012–15 delivered no widespread financial crisis, it is really only necessary to point to two factors: balance sheet strength and floating exchange rates. When foreign reserves are plentiful, countries have a natural buffer against capital outflows. And when currencies are floating, investors have no expectation of being paid out at a fixed rate, and countries themselves benefit from the shock-absorbing qualities of a flexible exchange rate. Both these factors were the legacy of the two decades of crisis that developing countries had suffered in the 1980s and 1990s. As we discovered in earlier chapters, the lessons of these crises were, simply put, to build strong balance sheets and not try to defend indefensible currencies. By the 2010s, developing countries had moved 180 degrees from their situation in the late 1990s. Whereas the tendency back then had been to peg currencies against the dollar without sufficient reserves to sustain those pegs, countries were now allowing their currencies to float and were accumulating plenty of reserves, too. Developing countries have thus proved themselves to be significantly more adept at navigating the volatility of global capital flows. And it is in that sense that one can describe emerging economies as having become crisis-proof. Of course, it is conceivable that future monetary tightening by the Fed will be dramatic enough to drain developing countries of their reserves. But by the standards of recent history, these countries are remarkably well protected.

It might be helpful to summarize the account so far. On the one hand, a marked change in the intellectual climate has led to vocal expressions of dissatisfaction with unrestricted capital mobility, China's voice being the most prominent. But on the other hand, we are faced with a set of problems. First, developing countries with low savings ratios may not feel that they have the liberty to restrict the capital inflows on which they depend to grow. Second, the idea that emerging economies might be crisis-proofed these days might make them less worried about global capital mobility, and so less inclined to consider capital controls, if they feel they are better protected against its worst effects. And finally, not too many people have confidence that controlling capital flows can be effective in the long run.

It is possible to give tentative answers to these problems. Countries with low savings/GDP ratios may well need external financing to support growth; but that doesn't necessarily mean they are better off with *any* kind of financing. The right approach for them may simply be to adjust their policy frameworks in ways that prioritize inflows of FDI, and deprioritize everything else. Equally, countries that feel crisis-proof may still want to avoid the economic volatility produced by global capital mobility, even if they have reduced their exposure to financial crisis. In other words, they may still have an interest in using capital controls. A deeper problem for the argument in favor of restricting capital mobility lies in the fact that such restrictions are difficult to police. After all, the postwar Bretton Woods regime, which relied on limiting capital movements, broke down after less than thirty years. What follows is therefore not an attempt to argue that the world will somehow find a way to make capital controls stick. Instead, it is an attempt to show that, for better or worse, a global monetary system more shaped by China is likely to include more restrictions on the global movement of capital and a more state-centered path toward growth.

Belts, Roads, and China's Money

The world economy is substantially China shaped these days. In 2016, China alone was responsible for nearly 40 percent of global GDP growth. And on average during the five years between 2012 and 2016, China's contribution to global GDP growth was 36 percent. For comparison: the last time the United States was so influential in delivering global GDP growth was in the second half of the 1990s.

One way of summing up the situation now faced by developing countries is that while the *capital* account of their balance of payments—the availability of external financing—remains heavily determined by what the U.S. Fed does, the *current* account—exports and imports—is increasingly shaped by China. Yet this allocation of roles between China and the United States may be in the process of changing—or at least it is becoming much more tempting to argue that China is emerging not just as a driver of economic outcomes in the developing world but also as a supplier of funding.

China's emerging role as a source of external financing for developing countries lies most visibly in the rollout of its One Belt, One Road investment program or, as it is more commonly known now, the Belt and Road Initiative (BRI).[16] The BRI is China's strategy to "promote connectivity" among a group of countries featured in two separate initiatives announced by President Xi Jinping in 2013. One is the Silk Road Economic Belt, aimed at boosting trade across the Eurasian landmass that connects China with Europe. The other is its sister project, a so-called 21st Century Maritime Silk Road, which aims to strengthen sea-lane connectivity among China's trading partners. These two initiatives constituting the BRI have in turn a loose relationship with economic corridors that have been announced between China and most of South Asia. Of these, the most important by far is the China-Pakistan Economic Corridor (CPEC), to which China has already committed some $60 billion for an array of projects, including power plants, roads, railways, dams, industrial zones, and, critically, the development of the port at Gwadar in southern Pakistan, near the border with Iran. The scale of China's financial muscle here is captured simply by understanding that $60 billion is equal to nearly a quarter of Pakistan's 2016 GDP, which was just below $280 billion.

Chinese officials try to dismiss the idea that there is a geopolitical game going on here, but obviously it is tempting to see this as the seed of a "Pax Sinica"—a huge China-friendly economic space that is, depending on one's view, a "community of shared interests" or a "zone of deference." Some Chinese analysts have talked about the BRI as being the "second opening" after the first one, post-1979, overseen by Deng Xiaoping, which turned China into what it is today. And in the couple of years following the announcement of the BRI, China moved to mobilize hefty financial resources to support investments in infrastructure projects for the countries involved. The most visible of these moves have been the creation of the Asian Infrastructure Investment Bank, set up with an initial capital base of $100 billion (of which $40 billion came from China), which can lend up to two-and-a-half times its capital, and the establishment of the New Development Bank (or "BRICS bank"), with initial capital of $50 billion (of which $20 billion came from China). But there are plenty of others: a new Silk Road Fund with $40 billion of capital; a new subsidiary of CIC, China's sovereign wealth fund, called CIC Capital, with a target of $100 billion; and recapitalizations, each worth close to $50 billion, in 2015 of China Development Bank and the Export-Import Bank of China, with the explicit goal of financing China's BRI ambitions.

Since the BRI has become such a central preoccupation of Beijing—in October 2017, it was incorporated into the Communist Party's constitution—there undoubtedly will be more initiatives and grand projects to come, even though a Chinese effort to restrict capital outflows from late 2016 caused a slowdown in foreign lending and investments related to the BRI.[17] The total amounts that have been assembled so far may not be globally game-changing, but this is still a story worth watching. There is no explicit list of countries eligible to be part of the BRI, and China's financial exposure beyond anywhere that could remotely be interpreted as part of a modern Silk Road has already grown sharply. According to the World Bank, for example, China is now the Kenyan government's largest foreign bilateral creditor.[18] And since 2007, official Chinese lenders have supplied Latin America with some $135 billion in external financing.[19] Overall, China has emerged as a reasonably serious competitor to the United States when it comes to flows of outbound FDI. Data from the United Nations Conference on Trade and Development show that China's outflow of FDI was $183 billion in 2016, a sum second only to the United States' outflow of $299 billion.

China's growth model is heavily reliant on a banking system that is largely state-owned; on economic activism by local governments, particularly when it comes to investment in infrastructure; and on a substantial role for state-owned enterprises in many areas of the economy: telecommunications, transport, coal, and metals, for example. These are precisely the areas in which China's expertise will be shared with other countries in the context of the BRI.

One question worth asking, then, is whether the greater role for the state that characterizes Chinese economic policymaking could be echoed in the future by other developing countries. China explicitly declares a goal of being a model for other countries, and it is tempting to see how countries might adopt a more China-like emphasis on a relatively expanded role for the state. The most likely candidate for more state activism in economic policy is infrastructure. This played a huge role in China's growth: between 2006 and 2016, infrastructure spending accounted for about 14 percent of China's GDP growth.

Back to the Future, Part 2

It is almost universally acknowledged that the developing world could do with more and better infrastructure. In Indonesia, the cost of shipping a container from Padang to Jakarta is some three times the cost of getting the same container from Jakarta to Singapore, an almost identical distance. Brazilian soybean farmers must spend a quarter of their income getting crops to Santos, the country's main port; Iowan farmers spend a tiny fraction of that.[20] To compound the problem, it seems clear that considerably fewer resources are devoted to infrastructure than was the case in the past. In developing countries, by one estimate, the stock of public capital has fallen from a late 1980s peak of around 130 percent of GDP to a level nearer 85 percent today.[21]

The point here is that infrastructure-led growth overwhelmingly tends to be an endeavor of the public sector. Several reasons exist for this. One is that infrastructure investment tends to require large up-front costs but delivers returns only over a very long payback period. Another is that the returns from an infrastructure project don't necessarily accrue only to the investor but to society as a whole. A number of infrastructure projects also tend to have the properties of natural monopolies: high fixed costs require a large customer base to make investment worthwhile, and so providing some public utilities—water and electricity, for example—might be more practically done by a single supplier.

Let's imagine that we encounter more threats to economic globalization in the coming years. This is not an unreasonable concern in a world in which trade liberalization seems to have lost its appeal for some countries. In that kind of world, it is easy to imagine how infrastructure-led growth might seem attractive as an effective way to raise income levels. The usual argument is that infrastructure spending has two separate effects on income. One is the immediate boost to GDP growth that is generated by an increase in investment spending. The economic consequences of this "demand" effect can by analyzed in terms of its role as a "fiscal multiplier," just as with any other public spending. Another effect is longer term, because of the increase in productive capacity that is supposed to result from better roads, faster trains, bigger ports, more reliable power supplies, cleaner water, and broader wireless access. This can be thought of as the "supply" effect.

As an aside, it is worth pointing out that there are plenty of reasons to be skeptical about the impact of infrastructure investment on growth. A 2014 IMF paper, for example, concludes that public investment drives have a small positive and instantaneous effect on economic growth but little long-run impact.[22] And by some accounts, the causation actually works the other way around: in Korea and Taiwan, for example, infrastructure pushes were a response to congestion caused by several years of rapid growth. In 1967, for example, Korea's president Park Chung-hee announced a major national reconstruction plan largely because of the infrastructure shortages that were exposed after a period of very rapid growth in the mid-1960s.

Even if one doesn't really know whether infrastructure spending contributes significantly to economic growth, it is easy to see how the logic of investing in infrastructure might become appealing to developing country policymakers in a world in which China's evident success takes on the status of a model for other countries. That appeal might be greater because public debt ratios in many developing countries are, by historical standards, still relatively low. That is the legacy of the balance sheet strengthening with which many developing countries responded to the crises in the 1980s and 1990s, as discussed in chapter 3.

If China becomes a model for the benefits that public investment in infrastructure can deliver to a developing country, it might be possible to connect this with the idea of a world in which restrictions on capital mobility become more commonplace. This would be a truly China-shaped world, gathering together the two parts of the possible Beijing Consensus described earlier in this chapter: the role of the state in supporting growth and the role of the state in restricting capital mobility.

So what is the connection between a more infrastructure-reliant growth model and more widespread restrictions on global capital mobility? The answer lies in the stock of foreign exchange reserves that now sit heavily on developing countries' balance sheets.

Countries accumulated reserves as part of an effort to wrap up warmly against inclement financial weather. The problem is that there is no coherent way of saying "enough is enough" when it comes to accumulating reserves. Even if a country can repay its short-term debt several times over, there will still be an incentive to accumulate more reserves if other countries are doing so. If one country continues to accumulate reserves in an effort to stop its currency from strengthening too much, then other countries could suffer a competitive disadvantage unless they build up more reserves themselves. Another way of making this point is to consider things from the point of view of sovereign creditworthiness: if buying reserves makes a country more creditworthy, then other countries might have an incentive to do the same. In this sense, international finance contains within it some of the logic of an arms race. The fact that a superpower can already destroy swaths of the planet with its existing stock of nuclear weapons may not prevent it from acquiring more if its adversary is doing so. Reserves accumulation might have some similar features.

At the same time, the accumulation of reserves by developing countries may seem strange in a world of more floating exchange rates. In a way, having abundant reserves is a *substitute* for having a floating currency, and vice versa. The original advice to countries that they ought to buy more reserves was conceived in the late 1990s in an era still characterized largely by pegged exchange rates. The idea was that reserves were needed to make those pegs sustainable. But if a country is allowing its currency to float, then in principle at least reserves aren't needed. The float is a commitment to allowing the *prices* of a currency to vary in order to stabilize the balance of payments, and this somewhat erodes the need to have *quantities* of dollars to protect the balance of payments.

This excess of protection that developing countries have these days—possessing *both* large quantities of reserves *and* floating exchange rates—might open up a way of thinking about how foreign exchange reserves might be used in the future to support infrastructure-led development. A China-shaped world can be imagined in which capital controls get further destigmatized. In that world, it might be possible to imagine countries more willing to use their foreign exchange reserves as a source of funding for domestic infrastructure projects.

Conceivably, a couple of different factors might destigmatize the use of capital controls. One is time. With China having set its course toward "managed convertibility," with India following suit, and with the IMF having opened the door to the use of CFMs, it may just be a question of sitting and waiting to see more policymakers feel comfortable about introducing capital controls to help deal with the prospect of excessive inflows. One suspects that the closer China edges toward a position of influence in shaping the rules and norms of the international monetary system, the more it will reassert its view that the "wise" policymaker has a legitimate role to play in separating the good from the bad when it comes to global capital movements.

A global set of rules regarding capital controls might be another means of eroding the stigma that they still attract. One proposal along these lines sets up a comparison between the global rules governing trade in goods with those that might be used to govern trade in capital. Just as we have a World Trade Organization that allows countries to impose tariffs and challenge anticompetitive practices by trading partners, some argue that the world should develop an institution that legitimizes and supervises the use of protection against excessive capital flows.[23]

These two paths toward the destigmatization of capital controls might both be necessary. If a new set of Bretton Woods–like rules on the regulation of capital flows will indeed see the light of day, it will certainly take time to get there. But if this is an imaginable future, we will have come something like full circle. Before the 1970s, financing for developing countries came largely from official sources, as global capital flows were heavily restricted under the Bretton Woods regime and as the state played a decisive role in shaping domestic economic outcomes. A Beijing Consensus could lead us in the future to something not too dissimilar. When John Maynard Keynes spoke to the House of Lords in 1944 about the new Bretton Woods arrangements, he said: "Not merely as a feature of the transition, but as a permanent arrangement, the plan accords to every member government the explicit right to control all capital movements. What used to be a heresy is now endorsed as orthodox."[24] Indeed: the heresy, to Washington, of restricting capital movements in the 1980s and 1990s could be on its way to becoming a China-shaped orthodoxy.

Notes

Introduction

1. John-Paul Rathbone, *The Sugar King of Havana: The Rise and Fall of Julio Lobo, Cuba's Last Tycoon* (London: Penguin Books, 2010), p. 74.

2. Hugh Thomas, *Cuba: A History* (London: Penguin Books, 1971), p. 327.

3. Kevin Grogan, "Cuba's Dance of the Millions: Examining the Causes and Consequences of Violent Price Fluctuations in the Sugar Market between 1919 and 1920," mimeo, University of Florida, 2004, p. 48.

4. Rathbone, *The Sugar King of Havana*, p. 76.

5. Leland Hamilton Jenks, *Our Cuban Colony: A Study in Sugar* (New York: Vanguard, 1928), p. 220.

6. Ibid., p. 229.

7. John Kenneth Galbraith, "Insanity of 1929 Repeats Itself," *Sunday Times*, October 25, 1987.

8. Royal Institute of International Affairs, *The Problem of International Investment: A Report by a Study Group of Members of the Royal Institute of International Affairs* (London: Oxford University Press, 1937), p. 221. Data are converted from sterling.

9. Author's calculations using data from the Maddison Project (http://www.ggdc.net/maddison/maddison-project/home.htm).

10. Catherine Schenk, *International Economic Relations since 1945* (London: Routledge, 2011), p. 80.

11. Carmen M. Reinhart, Vincent Reinhart, and Christoph Trebesch, "Global Cycles: Capital Flows, Commodities and Sovereign Defaults, 1815–2015," *American Economic Review: Papers and Proceedings* 106, no. 5 (2016), pp. 574–80.

12. John Williamson, "The Strange History of the Washington Consensus," *Journal of Post-Keynesian Economics* 27, no. 2 (2005), p. 196.

13. Ibid., p. 201.

14. Author's calculations based on updated and extended version of data set from Philip R. Lane and Gian Maria Milesi-Ferretti, "The External Wealth of Nations Mark II: Revised and Extended Estimates of Foreign Assets and Liabilities, 1970–2004," *Journal of International Economics* 73, no. 2 (2007), pp. 223–50.

15. Maurice Obstfeld, "International Finance and Growth in Developing Countries: What Have We Learned?," NBER Working Paper 14691 (Cambridge, Mass.: National Bureau of Economic Research, February 2009).

16. Hélène Rey, "Dilemma Not Trilemma: The Global Financial Cycle and Monetary Policy Independence," *Proceedings—Economic Policy Symposium—Jackson Hole, Federal Reserve of Kansas City Economic Symposium* (2013), pp. 285–333.

17. IMF, *The Liberalization and Management of Capital Flows: An Institutional View* (Washington, D.C.: International Monetary Fund, November 14, 2012).

18. John Maynard Keynes, "National Self-Sufficiency," quoted in Harold James, *The End of Globalization: Lessons from the Great Depression* (Harvard University Press, 2001), p. 197. Emphasis added.

19. Lothrop Stoddard, quoted in Barry Eichengreen, "The U.S. Capital Market and Foreign Lending, 1920–1955," in *Developing Country Debt and the World Economy*, edited by Jeffrey D. Sachs (University of Chicago Press, 1989), p. 120.

20. Royal Institute of International Affairs, *The Problem of International Investment*, p. 170.

21. Carlos Marichal, *A Century of Debt Crises in Latin America: From Independence to the Great Depression, 1820–1930* (Princeton University Press, 1989), p. 183.

22. Barry Eichengreen, "Historical Research on International Lending and Debt," *Journal of Economic Perspectives* 5, no. 2 (1991), p. 152.

23. Jeffry A. Frieden, *Global Capitalism: Its Fall and Rise in the Twentieth Century* (London: W. W. Norton, 2006), p. 141.

24. Royal Institute of International Affairs, *The Problem of International Investment*, p. 11.

25. Ibid., p. 10.

26. Ibid., p. 11.

Chapter 1

1. Denis Healey, *The Time of My Life* (London: Michael Joseph, 1989), p. 423.

2. Benjamin Wallace-Wells, "Giuliani's Policy Professor," *Washington Post*, October 26, 2007.

3. Karin Lissakers, *International Debt, the Banks, and U.S. Foreign Policy: A Staff Report for the U.S. Senate Committee on Foreign Relations* (U.S. Government Printing Office, 1977).

4. David Mulford, *Packing for India: A Life of Action in Global Finance and Diplomacy* (Washington, D.C.: Potomac Books, 2014), p. 104.

5. Michael Field, "The Oil Surplus," *Financial Times*, January 12, 1976.

6. Mulford, *Packing for India*, p. 106.

7. Richard Mattione, *OPEC's Investments and the International Financial System* (Brookings Institution Press, 1985), p. 65.

8. Geoffrey Bell, *The Euro-dollar Market and the International Financial System* (London: Macmillan, 1973), p. 8.

9. Paul Volcker, "The Recycling Problem Revisited," speech delivered at New York University, March 1, 1980.

10. Alan S. Blinder, "The Anatomy of Double-Digit Inflation in the 1970s," in *Inflation: Causes and Effects*, edited by Robert E. Hall (University of Chicago Press, 1982), pp. 261–82.

11. Federal Deposit Insurance Corporation, "The LDC Debt Crisis," p. 206 (https://www.fdic.gov/bank/historical/history/191_210.pdf).

12. H. A. Holley, *Developing Country Debt: The Role of the Commercial Banks*, Chatham House Papers 35 (London: Routledge and Kegan Paul, 1987), p. 5.

13. Karin Lissakers, *Banks, Borrowers and the Establishment: A Revisionist Account of the International Debt Crisis* (New York: Basic Books, 1991), p. 63.

14. Ibid., p. 56.

15. Jahangir Amuzegar, "Oil Exporters' Economic Development in an Interdependent World," IMF Occasional Paper 18 (Washington, D.C.: International Monetary Fund, 1983).

16. Alberto Chong and Florencio López-de-Silanes, "Privatization in Mexico," IADB Research Department Working Paper 513 (Washington, D.C.: Inter-American Development Bank, August 2004), p. 8.

17. Jeffry A. Frieden, *Debt, Development and Democracy: Modern Political Economy and Latin America* (Princeton University Press, 1991), p. 421.

18. Jeffry A. Frieden, "Third World Indebted Industrialization: International Finance and State Capitalism in Mexico, Brazil, Algeria and South Korea," *International Organization* 35, no. 3 (Summer 1981), p. 429.

19. Frieden, *Debt, Development and Democracy*, p. 155.

20. Douglas Tweedale, "Sweet Money Leaves Sour Aftertaste," *The Times*, September 25, 1984.

21. Robert Crumby and Richard Levich, "On the Definition and Magnitude of Recent Capital Flight," in *Capital Flight and Third World Debt,* edited by Donald R. Lessard and John Williamson (Washington, D.C.: Institute for International Economics, 1987), pp. 27–67.

22. Henry C. Wallich, "LDC Debt: To Worry or Not to Worry," remarks at the 59th Annual Meeting of the Bankers' Association for Foreign Trade, Boca Raton, Fla., June 1981, p. 9.

23. Pedro-Pablo Kuczynski, *Latin American Debt* (Johns Hopkins University Press, 1988), p. 51.

24. Group of Thirty, *The Outlook for International Bank Lending: A Survey of Opinion among Leading International Bankers* (New York: Group of Thirty, 1981), p. 20.

25. Carlos F. Diaz-Alejandro, "Latin American Debt: I Don't Think We Are in Kansas Anymore," *Brookings Papers on Economic Activity* 2 (1984), p. 340.

26. Sebastian Mallaby, *The Man Who Knew: The Life and Times of Alan Greenspan* (London: Bloomsbury, 2016), p. 232.

27. Federal Deposit Insurance Corporation, "The LDC Debt Crisis," p. 196.

Chapter 2

1. U.S. Central Intelligence Agency, "Poland, Hard Currency Default Looms," February 20, 1981, p. 1 (https://www.cia.gov/library/readingroom/docs/DOC_0000235202.pdf).

2. Capital flows data kindly supplied by the Institute of International Finance, Washington, D.C.

3. Lee C. Buchheit, "Cross-Border Lending: What's Different This Time?," *Northwestern Journal of International Law and Business* 16, no. 1 (Fall 1995), p. 45.

4. Alan Greenspan, *The Age of Turbulence* (London: Allen Lane, 2007), p. 155.

5. Capital flows data kindly supplied by the Institute of International Finance, Washington, D.C.

6. Walter Bagehot, *Lombard Street: A Description of the Money Market* (London: Kegan, Paul, 1878), p. 52.

7. Federal Deposit Insurance Corporation, "The LDC Debt Crisis," p. 207 (https://www.fdic.gov/bank/historical/history/191_210.pdf).

8. Karin Lissakers, *Banks, Borrowers and the Establishment: A Revisionist Account of the International Debt Crisis* (New York: Basic Books, 1991), p. 204.

9. A. D. Horne, "Debts Paid, Romania Says; Ceauşescu Announces Austerity's Result," *Washington Post,* April 14, 1989.

10. Paul Volcker and Toyoo Gyohten, *Changing Fortunes: The World's Money and the Threat to American Leadership* (New York: Times Books, 1992), p. 204.

11. William R. Cline, *International Debt Re-examined* (Washington, D.C.: Institute for International Economics, 1995), p. 209.

12. William R. Cline, "The Baker Plan and Brady Reformulation: An Evaluation," in *Dealing with the Debt Crisis*, edited by Ishrat Husain and Ishac Diwan (Washington, D.C.: World Bank, 1989), p. 180.

13. Eric N. Berg, "Citicorp Accepts a Big Loss Linked to Foreign Loans," *New York Times*, May 20, 1987.

14. Federal Deposit Insurance Corporation, "The LDC Debt Crisis," p. 196.

15. Philip R. Lane and Gian Maria Milesi-Ferretti, "The External Wealth of Nations Mark II: Revised and Extended Estimates of Foreign Assets and Liabilities, 1970–2004," *Journal of International Economics* 73, no. 2 (Washington, D.C.: International Monetary Fund, November 2007), pp. 223–50.

16. IMF, *The IMF's Approach to Capital Account Liberalization* (Washington, D.C.: International Monetary Fund, 2005), p. 47.

17. Oya Celasun, "The 1994 Currency Crisis in Turkey," World Bank Policy Research Working Paper WPS1913 (Washington, D.C.: World Bank, 1999), p. 4.

18. Carmen M. Reinhart and Kenneth S. Rogoff, *This Time Is Different: Eight Centuries of Financial Folly* (Princeton University Press, 2009), p. 1.

19. Quoted in Volcker and Gyohten, *Changing Fortunes*, p. 315.

20. Quoted in Jeffrey M. Chwieroth, *Capital Ideas: The IMF and the Rise of Financial Liberalization* (Princeton University Press, 2010), p. 148.

21. Paul Krugman, "Dutch Tulips and Emerging Markets," *Foreign Affairs* 74, no. 4 (July–August 1995), p. 36.

22. World Bank, *Asia: The Road to Recovery* (Washington, D.C.: World Bank, 1998), p. 2.

23. Stanley Fischer, "Exchange Rate Regimes: Is the Bipolar View Correct?," speech given on January 6, 2001, p. 13 (https://www.imf.org/en/News/Articles/2015/09/28/04/53/sp010601a).

24. A. Javier Hamann, "Exchange Rate-Based Stabilization: A Critical Look at the Stylized Facts," IMF Working Paper WP/99/132 (Washington, D.C.: International Monetary Fund, October 1999).

25. Peter Blair Henry, "Capital Account Liberalization: Theory, Evidence and Speculation," Federal Reserve Bank of San Francisco Working Paper 2007-32 (November 2006), p. 59.

26. Paul Blustein, *The Christening: Inside the Crisis That Rocked the Global Financial System and Humbled the IMF* (New York: Public Affairs Books, 2003), p. 56.

27. Graciela Kaminsky and Carmen Reinhart, "The Twin Crises: The Causes of Banking and Balance-of-Payments Problems," *American Economic Review* 89, no. 3 (June 1999), pp. 473–500.

28. Luc Laeven and Fabián Valencia, "Systemic Banking Crises Database: An Update," IMF Working Paper WP/12/163 (Washington, D.C.: International Monetary Fund, June 2012).

29. Michael M. Hutchison and Ilan Noy, "How Bad Are the Twins? Output Costs of Currency and Banking Crises," *Journal of Money, Credit and Banking* 37, no. 4 (2005), pp. 725–52.

30. Joseph Stiglitz, *Globalization and Its Discontents* (London: Allen Lane; New York: Penguin Press, 2002), p. 99.

31. Ibid., p. 102.

32. Martin Wolf, "No More Than a Blip," *Financial Times*, July 15, 1997.

Chapter 3

1. John Williamson, ed., *Latin American Adjustment: How Much Has Happened?* (Washington, D.C.: Institute for International Economics, 1990).

2. Ibid., p. 18.

3. Robert N. Seidel, "American Reformers Abroad: The Kemmerer Missions in South America, 1923–1931," *Journal of Economic History* 32, no. 2 (June 1972), p. 522.

4. Quoted in Seidel, "American Reformers Abroad," p. 524.

5. Peter Passell, "Dr. Jeffrey Sachs, Shock Therapist," *New York Times*, June 27, 1993.

6. Eliana Cardoso and Anne Helwege, *Latin America's Economy: Diversity, Trends and Conflicts* (Cambridge, Mass.: MIT Press, 1992), p. 85.

7. Harry Johnson, *The World Economy at the Crossroads* (Oxford: Clarendon Press, 1965), p. 75.

8. Werner Baer, "Import Substitution and Industrialisation in Latin America: Experiences and Interpretations," *Latin American Research Review* 7, no. 1 (Spring 1972), pp. 95–122.

9. Johnson, *The World Economy at the Crossroads*, p. 83.

10. Helena Tang and Ann Harrison, "Trade Liberalization: Why So Much Controversy," in *Economic Growth in the 1990s: Learning from a Decade of Reform* (Washington, D.C.: World Bank, 2005), p. 186.

11. Rüdiger Dornbusch, "The Case for Trade Liberalization in Developing Countries," *Journal of Economic Perspectives* 6, no. 1 (Winter 1992), p. 79.

12. Ibid., p. 75.

13. Mumtaz Hussain Shah and Yahya Khan, "Trade Liberalization and FDI Inflows in Emerging Economies," *Business and Economic Review* 8, no. 1 (2016), p. 36.

14. UNCTAD, *World Investment Report, 2002* (Geneva: United Nations), p. 154.

15. Ayhan M. Kose, Eswar Prasad, Kenneth Rogoff, and Shang-Jin Wei, "Financial Globalization: A Reappraisal," NBER Working Paper 12484 (Cambridge, Mass.: National Bureau of Economic Research, August 2006), p. 3.

16. Eswar Prasad, Kenneth Rogoff, Shang-Jin Wei, and M. Ayhan Kose, "Effects of Financial Globalization on Developing Countries: Some Empirical Evi-

dence," IMF Occasional Paper 220 (Washington, D.C.: International Monetary Fund, 2003).

17. Data kindly supplied by the Institute of International Finance, Washington, D.C.

18. Robert Cull and Maria Soledad Martinez Peria, "Foreign Bank Participation in Developing Countries: What Do We Know about the Drivers and Consequences of This Phenomenon?," World Bank Policy Research Working Paper 5398 (Washington, D.C.: World Bank, August 2010), p. 2.

19. Kose and others, "Financial Globalization."

20. John Williamson, "The Strange History of the Washington Consensus," *Journal of Post-Keynesian Economics* 27, no. 2 (Winter 2005), p. 198.

21. Ibid., p. 201.

22. Williamson, *Latin American Adjustment*, p. 26.

23. Lawrence H. Summers, "International Financial Crises: Causes, Prevention and Cures," *American Economic Review* 90, no. 2 (May 2000), p. 3.

24. Joseph Stiglitz, *Globalization and Its Discontents* (London: Allen Lane; New York: Penguin Press, 2002), p. 102.

25. Sebastian Edwards, introduction to *Capital Controls and Capital Flows in Emerging Economies: Policies, Practices and Consequences*, edited by Sebastian Edwards (University of Chicago Press, 2004), p. 9.

26. IMF, *The IMF's Approach to Capital Account Liberalization* (Washington, D.C.: International Monetary Fund, 2005), p. 32.

27. Rawi Abdelal, "The IMF and the Capital Account," in *Reforming the IMF for the 21st Century*, edited by Edwin M. Truman (Washington, D.C.: Institute for International Economics, 2006), pp. 185–197.

28. Stanley Fischer, "Capital Account Liberalization and the Role of the IMF," speech given on September 19, 1997 (http://www.imf.org/en/News/Articles/2015/09/28/04/53/sp091997).

29. Michel Camdessus, "Capital Account Liberalization and the Role of the Fund," speech given on March 9, 1998 (https://www.imf.org/en/News/Articles/2015/09/28/04/53/sp030998).

30. José De Gregorio, Sebastian Edwards, and Rodrigo O. Valdés, "Controls on Capital Inflows: Do They Work?," *Journal of Development Economics* 63, no. 1 (2000), p. 64.

31. Ibid., p. 70.

32. Edward A. Gargan, "Premier of Malaysia Spars with Currency Dealer," *New York Times*, September 22, 1997.

33. David Wessel and Darren McDermott, "Mahathir Attacks Speculation and Soros, Who Returns Fire," *Wall Street Journal*, September 22, 1997.

34. Robert E. Rubin and Jacob Weisberg, *In an Uncertain World: Tough Choices from Wall Street to Washington* (New York: Random House, 2003), p. 257.

35. Paul Blustein, *The Christening: Inside the Crisis That Rocked the Global Financial System and Humbled the IMF* (New York: Public Affairs Books, 2003), p. 48.

36. Nicolas Magud and Carmen Reinhart, "Capital Controls: An Evaluation," in *Capital Controls and Capital Flows in Emerging Economies: Policies, Practices and Consequences*, edited by Sebastian Edwards (University of Chicago Press, 2004), p. 647.

37. Martin Feldstein, "A Self-Help Guide for Emerging Markets," *Foreign Affairs* 78, no. 2 (March–April 1999), pp. 93–109.

38. Alan Greenspan, "Currency Reserves and Debt," speech given on April 29, 1999.

39. Williamson, "The Strange History of the Washington Consensus," p. 195.

40. IMF, "Public Debt In Emerging Markets: Is It Too High?," in *World Economic Outlook*, September 2003 (Washington, D.C.: International Monetary Fund, 2003), p. 118.

41. Institute of International Finance, *Capital Flows to Emerging Markets* report, June 5, 2017.

42. These calculations follow a line of thinking developed in Lawrence H. Summers, "Reflections on Global Account Imbalances and Emerging Markets Reserve Accumulation" (L. K. Jha Memorial Lecture, March 24, 2006). The IMF these days has a rather sophisticated framework for assessing reserves adequacy in emerging economies. It is only for the sake of simplicity that this narrower definition is being used. The IMF's approach is described here: http://www.imf.org/external/np/spr/ara/.

Chapter 4

1. John Williamson, "Is Brazil Next?," International Economics Policy Brief PB 02-7 (Washington, D.C.: Institute for International Economics, August 2002), p. 12.

2. Carmen M. Reinhart, Vincent Reinhart, and Christoph Trebesch, "Global Cycles: Capital Flows, Commodities and Sovereign Defaults, 1815–2015," *American Economic Review: Papers and Proceedings* 106, no. 5 (2016), pp. 574–80. The online appendix is located at https://assets.aeaweb.org/assets/production/articles-attachments/aer/app/10605/P2016_1014_app.pdf.

3. David S. Jacks, "From Boom to Bust: A Typology of Real Commodity Prices in the Long Run," NBER Working Paper 18874 (Cambridge, Mass.: National Bureau of Economic Research, March 2013).

4. Citi GPS, *China and Emerging Markets* (New York: Citi, 2012).

5. This excludes Saudi Arabia and the rest of the countries in the Gulf Cooperation Council. Countries included in this aggregate are Argentina, Brazil, Chile, Colombia, Ecuador, Egypt, Ghana, Indonesia, Nigeria, Peru, Russia,

South Africa, Uruguay, and Venezuela. Of course, it is understood that the population of commodity-exporting developing countries is larger than this.

6. Citi GPS, *China and Emerging Markets.*

7. Ibid.

8. Arthur Kroeber, *China's Economy: What Everyone Needs to Know* (Oxford University Press, 2016), p. 83.

9. Long Guoqiang, "China's Policies on FDI: Review and Evaluation," in *Does Foreign Direct Investment Promote Development?*, edited by Theodore H. Moran, Edward M. Graham, and Magnus Blomström (Washington, D.C.: Institute for International Economics, April 2005), p. 327.

10. Kroeber, *China's Economy*, p. 53.

11. Zhou Xiaochuan, "On Savings Ratio," address at the High Level Conference hosted by the Central Bank of Malaysia, Kuala Lumpur, February 10, 2009 (https://www.bis.org/review/r090327b.pdf).

Chapter 5

1. Evan Osnos, "Boom Doctor: Can the Chinese Miracle Continue without Reform?," *New Yorker*, October 11, 2010.

2. Justin Yifu Lin, "Why I Do Not Support Full Capital Account Liberalization," *China Economic Journal* 8, no. 1 (2015), pp. 86–93.

3. See chapter 1.

4. Zhou Xiaochuan, "Statement by the Honorable Zhou Xiaochuan, Governor of the IMF for China to the Thirty-First Meeting of the International Monetary and Financial Committee," Washington, D.C., April 18, 2015 (https://www.imf.org/External/spring/2015/imfc/statement/eng/chn.pdf).

5. David Lubin, "What the SDR Really Means for China," *beyondbrics* (blog), *Financial Times*, October 27, 2015 (https://www.ft.com/content/8d8338d7-eda9-34d5-9a71-a44cdcff9043).

6. Tom Lauricella and John Lyons, "Currency Wars: A Fight to Be Weaker," *Wall Street Journal*, September 29, 2010.

7. Marcos Chamon and Márcio Garcia, "Capital Controls in Brazil: Effective?," paper presented at the 15th Jacques Polak Annual Research Conference Hosted by the International Monetary Fund, Washington, D.C., November 2014 (https://www.imf.org/external/np/res/seminars/2014/arc/pdf/chamon_garcia.pdf).

8. Eswar S. Prasad, "Some New Perspectives on India's Approach to Capital Account Liberalization," NBER Working Paper 14658 (Cambridge, Mass.: National Bureau of Economic Research, January 2009.

9. Rakesh Mohan, Michael Debabrata Patra, and Muneesh Kapur, "The International Monetary System: Where Are We and Where Do We Need to Go?," IMF Working Paper WP/13/224 (Washington, D.C.: International Monetary Fund, November 2013).

10. Ibid., p. 26.

11. Ibid., p. 26.

12. Quoted in Eswar Prasad, *The Dollar Trap: How the U.S. Dollar Tightened its Grip on Global Finance* (Princeton University Press, 2014), p. 198.

13. Anton Korinek, "The New Economics of Capital Controls Imposed for Prudential Reasons," IMF Working Paper WP/11/298 (Washington, D.C.: International Monetary Fund, December 2011), p. 4.

14. IMF, *The Liberalization and Management of Capital Flows: An Institutional View* (Washington, D.C.: International Monetary Fund, November 14, 2012).

15. Michael Gavin, Ricardo Hausmann, and Ernesto Talvi, "Saving Behaviour in Latin America: Overview and Policy Issues," Inter-American Development Bank Working Paper 346 (Washington, D.C.: Inter-American Development Bank, May 1997).

16. David Lubin, "China Casts Cloud—and Silver Lining—over EM," *beyondbrics* (blog), *Financial Times*, September 29, 2015 (https://www.ft.com/content/7120497a-9811-3e09-8443-ac392ed6d912).

17. Gabriel Wildau and Ma Nan, "China's Drive for Modern-Day Silk Road Pulls into the Slow Lane," *Financial Times*, May 11, 2017.

18. Apurva Sanghi and Dylan Johnson, "Deal or No Deal: Strictly Business for China in Kenya?," World Bank Policy Research Working Paper 7614 (Washington, D.C.: World Bank, March 2016).

19. Kevin P. Gallagher and Margaret Myers, "China–Latin America Finance Database" (https://www.thedialogue.org/map_list/).

20. This is drawn from Citi GPS, Jason Channell, and others, *Infrastructure for Growth* (New York: Citi, 2016).

21. Ibid., p. 9.

22. Andrew M. Warner, "Public Investment as an Engine of Growth," IMF Working Paper WP/14/148 (Washington, D.C.: International Monetary Fund, August 2014).

23. Olivier Jeanne, Arvind Subramanian, and John Williamson, *Who Needs to Open the Capital Account?* (Washington, D.C.: Peterson Institute for International Economics, April 2012).

24. Quoted in Benjamin J. Cohen, *The Future of Money* (Princeton University Press, 2004), p. 107.

Index